Pathlight to Praise

150 Days of Psalms

Kristi Neace, MDiv.

Crossover Books, a division of Pelican Ventures, LLC
www.pelicanbookgroup.com PO Box 1738 *Aztec, NM * 87410
Crossover Books and the Cross-and-Sun logo is a trademark of Pelican Ventures, LLC

Publishing History
First Crossover Books Edition, 2024
Electronic Edition ISBN 978-1-5223-0470-8
Paperback Edition ISBN 978-1-5223-0479-1
Published in the United States of America

Dedication

To my Heavenly Father. Thank You for this answer to many prayers. Without You, this book would have never come to fruition.

To my sweet husband, Rick. Your patience, love, and encouragement have kept me believing. Thank you for being my steady.

DAY 1

PSALM 1:1-2

"Blessed is the man who does not walk in the counsel of the wicked or stand in the way of sinners or sit in the seat of mockers. But his delight is in the law of the LORD, and on his law he meditates day and night."

~*~

[Psalm 1 is a comparison/contrast of the ways of the wicked and the righteous. These words remind the reader that those who follow God must display qualities of righteousness that will set them apart from all the rest.]

I remember in high school all the different classes of students. First, there were the Brainiacs. They were the Valedictorians, the math club wizzes, and those who received all the scholarships. Then came the popular people who drove fancy cars, dated cheerleaders or football players, and seemingly had all the clothes, money, and notoriety. The corner kids were those individuals hanging together across the street who typically were the smokers, the leather-wearing, cowboy boot stomping, class skipping individuals who never seemed to fit it. And, finally, there were the ordinaries. People like me who followed the rules, didn't cause a ruckus, completed all assignments...well, most, and blended in when possible. We were all members of the same school, but each of us had adapted to certain categories of people.

In Psalm 1, the author is contrasting the lives of "sinners" with the lives of the "righteous". He points to the fact that each of us has a choice in life. We can choose either to run with those of the world or stay rooted in God. Though following the world may be the easier choice, this passage reminds us that individuals who delight in the Lord and in His law (the entirety of His revelation) receive the blessings of God.

The writer elaborates on these blessings in verse 3 where he writes, "He is like a tree planted by streams of water, which yields its fruit in season and whose leaf does not wither. Whatever he does prospers."

The tree has a root base which goes deep within the ground to drink up the nourishment from the stream. A believer who plants deep roots in God through faith, prayer and Bible study, is nourished by His never-ending, eternal stream of living water. Therefore, if one stays in step with the Trinity, then he or she will not only be productive, spiritually healthy, and bear spiritual fruit, but he or she will be a blessing to others by providing shade, shelter, and sustenance in the form of encouragement, strength, and spiritual nourishment.

Today, may we examine our lives and see where we fit in. Are we more like those who tend to follow the world, or do we walk with those who are rooted in

God's truth? Let's choose to be like the tree!

WHAT IS GOD REVEALING TO YOU ABOUT YOUR ROOTS TODAY? ARE THERE ANY CHANGES THAT NEED TO BE MADE?

DAY 2

*"Why do the nations conspire and the peoples plot in vain?
The kings of the earth take their stand and the rulers gather
together against the LORD and against his Anointed One."*

~*~

[Chapter 2 was written for the coronation of
Davidic kings, and in consideration of God's
covenant with David. However, it would later
become prophetic words of judgment and would
point to a future redemption of God's people through
Jesus Christ.]

In this passage we see actions taken against God
and His Anointed. Nations, kings, and people were
rising up, usurping their authority, flexing their
muscles, and going their own way.

They, like foolish men and women before them,
were not seeking after God but relying on their own
limited strength and knowledge and were trying to
break free from God's ultimate and sovereign rule, His
plans, and His provision. In essence, they were
thumbing their nose at God.

However, in verses 4 and 5, we read that God

scoffs or laughs at, rebukes, and then terrifies them in His anger. He has the last say, and though God is long-suffering towards mankind and wishes that none perish, there will come a time when He says, "enough!". Man may think he is in control; a king or government may perceive that they are in a seat of power, but if they set their face against the Lord, wrath is ultimately what they will receive.

Before His patience comes to its end, we must turn back to and seek the Lord.

HAVE YOU EVER TRIED TO LIVE BY YOUR OWN STRENGTH INSTEAD OF RELYING ON GOD? WHAT WAS THE OUTCOME? WHAT CAN YOU DO TODAY TO TRUST GOD MORE FULLY?

DAY 3

"Many are saying of me, 'God will not deliver him.' But you are a shield around me, O LORD; you bestow glory on me and lift up my head. To the LORD I cry aloud, and he answers me from his holy hill. I lie down and sleep; I wake up again, because the LORD sustains me."

~*~

[In chapter 3, King David is fleeing from his own son, Absalom, who is conspiring to take over the throne.].]

It is most likely that you've never had to flee from your own child, but this was David's situation. We can imagine it was painful, frustrating, embarrassing, and every other emotion that comes to mind. Yet, David knew he could count on God to not abandon him when everyone else had.

Psalm 3 reminds us that God is with us even in the most dark and difficult moments. David likens God to a shield around him, something, or more like *Someone*, who would protect him from weapons forged against him. David understood that he could call upon the Lord, and the Lord would hear. God is not too far away or so distant that He does not care what we are encountering here on earth.

David also realized he could allow himself to lie down and find rest knowing the Lord would watch over him like a mother watches her child.

In this passage, there are so many promises to cling to when we are walking through our own difficulties. Remember, God protects, He hears, answers, and sustains. He truly *is* a good and loving God!

RECALL A TIME WHEN GOD DEMONSTRATED HIS LOVE AND CARE FOR YOU DURING DIFFICULT SEASONS.

DAY 4

"In your anger do not sin; when you are on your beds, search your hearts and be silent. Offer right sacrifices and trust in the LORD."

~*~

[This psalm is a prayer for relief from his slanderous enemies.]

The people had turned away from the Lord and had embraced delusions and false gods to try to find relief. They had forgotten that God's timetable and man's timetable, His ways and our ways, can be totally different.

In this passage, David rebukes them and calls out their sin. The people had allowed anger to take hold, so, David is urging them to consider their own reactions—to search their hearts and not to grumble, but to remain silent. There's a quote credited to Abraham Lincoln which says, "Better to remain silent and be thought a fool than to speak and to remove all doubt."

It is almost always best to remain quiet when we are angry and anxious, yet, is so difficult, especially when we are about to spew all the frustrations we've been harboring. But giving over to those frustrations is what brings us to the precipice of sin. Righteous anger isn't sinful, but when we grumble it's a slippery slope into becoming sinfully indignant and vengeful. David offers the people a righteous option: stay silent, offer (right) sacrifices, and trust in the Lord.

This is a great reminder for each of us. We are going to go through times when we cannot see God working. We may feel as if He's left the building, and the temptation will be to grumble, complain, and try and find another solution.

In those instances, let us put into practice these words. May we think over our problems, remain quiet, then give them to God and trust His provision. By doing so, we will be in a much better frame of mind and will prevent our hearts from sinning.

HAS GOD INSTRUCTED YOU TO BE QUIET IN A PARTICULAR SITUATION? WHAT HAPPENED AND HOW DID IT MAKE YOU FEEL?

DAY 5

PSALM 5:3

"In the morning, O Lord, you hear my voice; in the morning I lay my requests before you and wait in expectation."

~*~

[This psalm is a cry for help from those who spread untruths and malign David's character.]

Do you pray? When do you pray? Some may pray at night before bed. Others may pray before each meal or before leaving the house. And what and how do you pray?

David tells us in this passage that he was laying his requests out to the Lord in the morning. He was giving to God his anxious thoughts and then waiting in expectation for God to move on his behalf. He was starting his day with a humble trust in God.

David recognized the fact that God was and is the only One who could help him. David's enemies were telling lies and plotting against him, and he needed God to lead, to give him refuge, and to show him the way through the hardships.

We can take lessons from David. Why not start our day in prayer? Why not come in humble submission to

God and give Him our anxious thoughts, then wait expectantly for Him to move on our behalf? If David, a warrior king, saw a need for prayer, then there must be something to it. Why not give it a try?

"The prayer of a righteous man is powerful and effective." James 5:16b

WHAT TIME OF DAY DO YOU HAVE YOUR PRAYER TIME? IF IT'S LATER IN THE DAY, TRY TO SET ASIDE TIME FIRST THING IN THE MORNING. PUT GOD FIRST AND SEE WHAT EFFECT IT WILL HAVE ON YOUR DAY.

IF YOU'VE NOT YET SCHEDULED A SET TIME FOR DAILY PRAYER, TRY TO DO SO NOW. IF YOUR SCHEDULE MAKES THAT DIFFICULT, KEEP IN MIND THAT FIVE MINUTES EACH DAY IS BETTER THAN NO MINUTES.

DAY 6

"My soul is in anguish. How long, O LORD, how long?"

~*~

[Known as part of the seven penitential psalms, it was written during a time of great trouble for David, whether in illness or conflict.]
Chapter six is written in a time of great stress, and these words penned to paper by the psalmist resonate with us still today. The writer is asking God to have mercy; not to consume David in his time of weakness. He reminds God of His unfailing love, and the psalmist displays a steadfast confidence that God has heard his cries and will answer.

There are times in life when we are so burdened by illness or attacks or loss or hurt, that we cry out, "Why?" Yet the psalmist never asks such a question; rather he asks, "How long?" He understands that there is a beginning and, somewhere out there. an end to his suffering. He doesn't know exactly how long the suffering will continue, but he does know that God is both trustworthy and in control of the timetable.

This a good reminder to us. In our hour of need,

16

may we remember *Who* is still in control. Though we may not like the circumstances, through them we can be sure that God sees and hears our prayers. This season of hardship will pass eventually. In the meantime, if we keep our eyes on Him, we can endure victoriously.

HAVE YOU COME TO A PLACE WHERE YOU CAN TRUST GOD TOTALLY WITH THE OUTCOME? IF SO, CALL TO MIND THE WAY IT FELT IN THAT INITIAL MOMENT WHEN YOU COMPLETELY SURRENDERED TO GOD'S SOVEREIGNTY. IF NO, CONSIDER WHAT'S HOLDING YOU BACK FROM TRUSTING IN HIM COMPLETELY.

DAY 7

PSALM 7:9

"O righteous God, who searches minds and hearts, bring to an end the violence of the wicked and make the righteous secure."

~*~

[David appeals to God to enact justice upon his enemies.]

King Saul was determined to end David's life, but David was appealing to the Everlasting King to save him from his enemies.

In this beautiful prayer to the Lord, the psalmist repeats what he knows to be true—that God is righteous. He is faithful in His commitments to His people. The powerless look to Him for help and protection, and He delivers them. He is holy and good.

Next, David acknowledges that God searches the minds and hearts of every living being. This means that God not only knows your thoughts and mine, but also the thoughts of our enemies. Nothing takes Him by surprise, and that truth should give us comfort.

Finally, David makes his request to God to stop the madness and give him some relief. I think we can especially relate to this part of David's prayer as it reflects on all the events going on in our world today.

So, friend, whatever is causing us stress and worry, know that God sees our anxious thoughts, and He knows how He will answer. All you and I need to do is to go to Him in prayer, as David continually did, and lay out our petitions. God is good, and He will come to our defense.

WHERE IS YOUR WORRY TODAY? DO YOU BELIEVE GOD CAN ANSWER? DO YOU BELIEVE THAT GOD *will* ANSWER? CONSIDER YOUR ANSWER TO THOSE QUESTIONS AND THE REASONS BEHIND THOSE ANSWERS.

DAY 8

"O LORD, our Lord, how majestic is your name in all the earth! You have set your glory above the heavens. From the lips of children and infants you have ordained praise because of your enemies, to silence the foe and the avenger. When I consider your heavens, the work of your fingers, the moon and the stars, which you have set in place, what is mankind that you are mindful of him, the son of man that you care for him?"

~*~

[A praise of the Creator and admiration of His glory and greatness.]

The psalmist begins by acknowledging God as the great I AM, the holy One. "Lord" is a title or translation of the word Adonai, or Master.

Here, God's majestic creation is on display in the heavens. He has set everything in its place, and the enormity of the universe is simply mind-blowing when compared to a minuscule speck on earth called "man".

Thankfully, God is not so large or distant that He does not know us intimately. The Bible tells us that He knows the number of hairs on our head (Luke 12:7) He knows our thoughts and examines our ways. His desire is to have a personal relationship with each one of us.

Little children in their purity of heart recognize that there is a Creator, and they praise Him. If we look in Matthew 21:15-16, we find Jesus in the temple and children praising Him saying, Hosanna to the Son of David!" Even then, when the most religious men of all would not recognize the Messiah standing before them, children sang His praises.

Today, may we not forget Who God is. May we recognize the fact that the entire universe is in His control, and He still cares for us. May we be like children in our faith and simply trust that He is who He says He is.

DO YOU SEE GOD'S HANDIWORK WHEN YOU LOOK AT CREATION—THE CLOUDS, TREES, STARS? CONSIDER THE DELICATE BALANCE THAT KEEPS THE EARTH SPINNING ON ITS AXIS, AND PONDER THE FACT THAT GOD HOLDS YOU IN THE PALM OF HIS HAND.

DAY 9

PSALM 9:16

"The LORD is known by his justice; the wicked are ensnared by the work of their hands."

~*~

[A psalm of celebration for all the help and goodness of God.]

Some might look at the Old Testament stories and think He seems harsh and even irate, yet they fail to realize that God is holy and righteous; therefore, He must punish sin. He has a moral standard we often don't like or understand.

In this chapter, the psalmist is again lamenting over those who are coming against him. His focus is on the nations of people who collectively devise wicked schemes and ignore the needy. But even in his lamentation about the unjust, the author concludes that because of God's justness, the wicked will not triumph; ultimately, the Lord will avenge those who put their trust in Him.

We must remember that even when it seems as if the wicked have the upper hand, God has the last say. His justice is equal to His mercy, and so He will avenge in due time, and all will be judged according to his actions.

WHAT JUSTICE ARE YOU WAITING ON FROM GOD TODAY? RATHER THAN BEING CONSUMED BY THOUGHTS OF ANGER OR VENGEANCE, REST IN THE TRUTH THAT GOD'S JUSTICE IS AS EXACT AS HIS MERCY.

DAY 10

"In his pride the wicked does not seek him; in all his thoughts there is no room for God."

~*~

[A prayer of deliverance from prideful, wicked men.]

Pride is an ugly character trait. Unfortunately, it is something with which we all struggle from time to time. It's the "me first" attitude that puffs us up and demands our own way. Perhaps you've dealt with someone who is full of himself. Typically, a person full of pride does not find fault from within, but looks for shortcomings in everyone else, and that can be a difficult situation to handle.

The writer of Proverbs lists seven sins the Lord detests, one being a prideful look. (Proverbs 6:16-19) Further, it was pride that caused the angel Lucifer to fall out of fellowship with God and become the enemy with whom we are so acquainted today. (Ezekiel 28:17)

In this verse, the psalmist relates pride with wickedness and clarifies that the one (or ones) who are prideful have no room for God. Why? Because pride is a rejection of God's sovereignty. When we put our will, our ambition, our accomplishments above God, we put ourselves on the throne of our hearts.

What a good reminder for us today! May we repent of our sin of pride and recognize the fact that without God, we would cease to exist.

DO YOU STRUGGLE WITH PRIDE? IF SO, CONSIDER WHY IT IS DIFFICULT TO MAINTAIN A HUMBLE ATTITUDE AND TO RECOGNIZE GOD'S RIGHTFUL PLACE IN YOUR LIFE.

Day 11

PSALM 11:3

"When the foundations are being destroyed, what can the righteous do?"

~*~

[David is testifying to his unwavering faith in the Lord. He alone is David's refuge in times of trouble.]

Wow. This verse stuck out to me like a flag waving in the wind. When wickedness comes into power, the righteous can no longer depend on a world system where good prevails and evil is silenced.

If we cross-reference Psalm 82:5, we read this, "They know nothing, they understand nothing. They walk about in darkness; all the foundations of the earth are shaken."

These rulers were permitted by God, yet instead of ruling in wisdom and seeking after Him, they are devoid of any true understanding of moral issues or the moral order God's rule sustains. When these people are in the seat of authority, the whole world begins to crumble. Compare current times to those in which David speaks. Do the similarities strike you?

So, where does our hope lie? What do we do? Going back to Psalm 11:1, the psalmist says, "In the LORD I take refuge." He then describes how God will deal with them.

Back to 82:7-8 we read, "But you will die like mere men; you will fall like every other ruler. Rise up, O God, judge the earth, for all the nations are your inheritance." Yes, indeed, Lord. Rise up! This should be our heart cry today.

DO YOU PRAY FOR THE LEADERS WHO LEAD OUR NATION AND OTHERS AROUND THE WORLD? IF NOT, CONSIDER DOING SO. ASK THE LORD TO GIVE THEM A HEART AND WILL THAT IS CONFORMED TO HIS, FOR THEM TO HAVE THE WISDOM TO GOVERN JUSTLY AND WITH MERCY.

DAY 12

PSALM 12:6

"And the words of the LORD are flawless, like silver refined in a furnace of clay, purified seven times."

~*~

[A prayer of David for help when it seems as if all mankind was faithless and full of deceit.]

There are a lot of words flying around these days. Thanks to social media, everyone seems to have found their voice, and this is exactly what was happening in David's day.

Here in Chapter twelve, David has been experiencing the effects of backbiting, gossip, and the slander from others. Therefore, in verse 6, he is comparing the words of his critics to God's pure, holy, and righteous Word, which he likens to silver that has been purified seven times.

He goes on to say that God will protect His Word and those who follow its precepts. Jesus, God's Word made Flesh, has overcome death and the grave. God's Word, the Bible, has stood the passage of thousands of years. Men have tried to eliminate it, yet in their feeble attempts, the Bible has only grown stronger.

Bible preacher, evangelist, and theologian Charles Spurgeon once said, "The Bible has passed through the furnace of persecution, literary criticism, philosophic doubt, and scientific discovery, and has lost nothing but those human interpretations which clung to it as alloy to precious ore. The experience of saints has tried it in every conceivable manner, but not a single doctrine or promise has been consumed in the most excessive heat."[1]

God's Word stands. Though people come against it, try to malign it, destroy it, call it old-fashioned and out of touch, it is the standard by which we should live. David recognized this and he kept his mind set on God's truth versus man's attempts to destroy him with idle words. Such a good reminder to us today.

HOW DO YOU DEAL WITH THOSE WHO CRITICIZE YOUR FAITH OR GOD'S WORD? DO YOU FEEL EQUIPPED TO BE ABLE TO DEFEND HIM WITHOUT BRINGING UNNECESSARY OFFENSE TO THOSE WHOSE OPINIONS DIFFER?

---

[1] "Psalm 12," C.H. Spurgeon, https://www.blueletterbible.org/Comm/spurgeon_charles/to d/ps012.cfm.

DAY 13

PSALM 13:5-6

"But I trust in your unfailing love; my heart rejoices in your salvation. I will sing to the LORD, for he has been good to me."

~*~

[David was pleading with God for deliverance, perhaps from a debilitating illness that would give the enemy an upper hand.]

Do you give God praise even when you have not yet received your answer? Do you sing songs to God even in the midst of your trials?

I was whining to God and to my husband some time ago, about something with which I have struggled for years but have yet to receive an answer for. I know the answer is coming, however when God says wait for twenty plus years, the delay can become burdensome.

David was feeling the same way as he asked, "How long must I wrestle with my thoughts and every day have sorrow in my heart (Ps. 13:2a)?" But...

That word, *but*, says it all. *But* I will trust in You. *But*, I will trust in your timing. *But*, I will trust in your way. Although I have to wait for Your timing, I will rest in your presence. Why? Because You, Lord, have been good to me.

Friend, can you say the same? Has God been good to you? Then trust in Him. He knows your situation and your desires, and will move when the time is right, and in His way.

ARE YOU WAITING ON GOD TO ANSWER? WHAT HAS HELPED YOU BE PEACEFUL IN THE WAIT? IF YOU HAVEN'T BEEN PEACEFUL IN YOUR WAIT, TRY TO MAKE A LIST OF WAYS IN WHICH THE LORD HAS BEEN GOOD TO YOU. EVEN SIMPLE THINGS LIKE ENJOYING A LIGHT BREEZE ON A HOT DAY OR SPENDING TIME WITH FRIENDS — ALL THESE ARE BLESSINGS.

DAY 14

PSALM 14:1

"The fool says in his heart, 'There is no God.' They are corrupt, their deeds are vile; there is no one who does good."

~*~

[David is describing the foolishness of those who say there is no God.]

Have you ever talked to an atheist? I once had a long conversation with a person who could not, or would not believe there is a God. Each time I brought up a point or characteristic of the Lord, he would try to counter me with Darwinian philosophy and atheistic ideas. When the debate was said and done, we parted with mutual respect, but I had a deep sense of sadness for this one who continued to put more faith in an untruth than in a God Who could save.

In this psalm, David is describing the folly of the one who believes in his or her heart that there is no God. He describes their thinking as corrupt and goes on to say, "there is no one who does good, not even one (vs. 3b)."

The Apostle Paul used these very words when he was writing his letter to the Romans. In Romans 3:10-

12 and talking about how both Jews and Gentiles are under sin, Paul writes, "As it is written: 'There is no one righteous, not even one; there is no one who understands, no one who seeks God. All have turned away, they have together become worthless; there is no one who does good, not even one.'"

THOSE ARE PRETTY HARSH WORDS, YET, THE TRUTH IS WE *ALL* HAVE SINNED AND FALLEN SHORT. THIS IS WHY YOU AND I NEEDED A PERFECT SAVIOR WHO WOULD COME AND DIE IN OUR PLACE, SO OUR SIN STAIN COULD BE WASHED AWAY.

HAVE YOU KNOWN SOMEONE WHO COMPLETELY REJECTS THE THOUGHT OF GOD? HOW DID YOU HANDLE THAT RELATIONSHIP?

DAY 15

"LORD, who may dwell in your sanctuary? Who may live on your holy hill? He whose walk is blameless and who does what is righteous..."

~*~

[Chapter 15 is a meditation of what characteristics a person should have in order to access God in His sanctuary.]

Have you ever been to the White House? I have a couple of times, and it is magnificent; however I remember feeling as if I didn't really belong there, like I was out of my league. It was pristine. The carpet was beautiful. The larger-than-life portraits were exquisite, and the room décor ornate. It was definitely dressed for a king...or a president, not as much for an average citizen and family. Yet, if the President of the United States would have popped his head out of one of the doorways, I would have completely melted. There was just something exciting about being in the house of the most powerful man in the nation.

In this psalm, David longed to be where God dwelt, and he considered, here, the type of

34

qualifications God would require for anyone who desired to come into His presence. The first two criteria he mentions are a blameless walk and doing what is righteous. Of course, we know that these are tough standards.

David goes on to say in verse three that the person should not be guilty of slander nor treat his neighbor unkindly, nor speak poorly towards his fellowman. James writes these words in James 1:26: "If anyone thinks he is religious and does not bridle his tongue but deceives his heart, this person's religion is worthless." In other words, what comes out of our mouth should reflect what is in our heart. If God has changed our heart, our words should be different. This is impossible, however, in our own strength because we are sinful people by nature. You and I need the Holy Spirit to help us speak in such a way that God gets the glory.

The Bible doesn't just leave us hanging with no hope. We are told how Jesus—God's perfect Son, came and died on a cross. He made the way, and if you and I put our faith and trust in Him, we are assured that one day we will dwell with Him forever in that holy place. Aren't you glad we have a Great High Priest who paid the price so that we might enjoy the benefits? Yes! Thank You, Jesus!

WHAT IS GOD WANTING FROM YOU TODAY? PERHAPS HE IS ASKING YOU TO MAKE CHANGES SO THAT YOU WILL BE READY TO DWELL WITH HIM FOREVER.

DAY 16

"I have set the LORD always before me. Because he is at my right hand, I will not be shaken."

~*~

[This psalm was David asking God for safekeeping, but also a statement of trust.]

God doesn't promise we will always be kept from dangerous or heartbreaking circumstances, but what He does promise is that He will be with us and walk right beside even when our world seems to be falling apart. We can have an unshakeable faith in times of shaking.

Throughout Chapter sixteen, David is offering praises to God. Even though he is facing great danger, he recognizes God as his source of protection and strength.

In verse eight, David purposefully places God first in his life, and because God is in His rightful place, David has confidence that he will not be shaken. For who (or what) can come against a person when the Lord is at the helm of his ship?

David goes on to list other blessings he will

experience such as a glad heart, praise, rest, joy, eternal pleasures, etc. Like David, if we put God first then we will experience an unexplainable inner joy and contentment. Those hardship and trials may come, but we, like David, can live with the full assurance that God will carry us through.

HOW HAS GOD STRENGTHENED YOU IN TIMES OF TROUBLE?

DAY 17

"Hear, O LORD, my righteous plea; listen to my cry. Give ear to my prayer—it does not rise from deceitful lips. May my vindication come from you, may your eyes see what is right. Though you probe my heart and examine me at night, though you test me, you will find nothing; I have resolved that my mouth will not sin."

~*~

[David appeals to the Lord for vindication from his enemies.]

These verses say so much about David's heart. First, he was again coming to God in a time of anguish. The mere fact that he keeps returning shows that his heart is set on God.

Second, David is confident in his approach to the Lord. He is sure that he has done no wrong in the situation at hand. We already know this from other passages such as Psalm 139:23-24, where David humbly asks God to: "Search me, O God, and know my heart; test me and know my anxious thoughts. See if there is any offensive way in me, and lead me in the way everlasting."

Third, David asks for vindication and for God to see what is right. David could have vindicated himself. He was a warrior king who fought many victorious battles. Yet, he wanted his vindication to come from the Lord. He recognizes the fact that God claims His right to vengeance (Deut. 32:35) and that only God's vengeance is just.

Finally, David again repeats his belief that he is "clean" before the Lord. He has gone so far to resolve or "fix his thought upon" not sinning with his words.

No wonder this king is described as a man after God's own heart. He was not perfect. Matter of fact, David sinned greatly against God in moments of weakness, yet we see how tender his heart is here, and how much he aimed to please the Lord and rely on Him.

We are not always going to walk a perfect Christian walk, but we can resolve today to continually pursue God; to ask God daily to examine our hearts and see if any wickedness resides there; to wait on God to take up our cause; and to fix ourselves securely in our relationship with Him.

HOW IS YOUR WALK WITH GOD? WOULD OTHERS CLASSIFY YOU AS A PERSON AFTER GOD'S OWN HEART?

DAY 18

PSALM 18:31-35

"For who is God besides the Lord? And who is the Rock except our God? It is God who arms me with strength and makes my way perfect. He makes my feet like the feet of a deer; he enables me to stand on the heights. He trains my hands for battle; my arms can bend a bow of bronze. You give me your shield of victory, and your right hand sustains me; you stoop down to make me great."

~*~

[Chapter 18 is a song of David reflecting over all God has done for him and how God has answered David's prayers, rescuing him from those who pursued him.]

Have you ever been to a museum, perhaps the Smithsonian, and observed a medieval suit of armor? The amount of metal on those things is incredible. I'm not sure how knights even stood up much less fought others proficiently. And, oftentimes, these soldiers would take little objects with them into battle for the hopeful purpose of good luck or protection.

In verses 31, David acknowledges THE God above all other gods. The nations surrounding worshipped all types of named gods, but they were just idols of stone, metal, or wood. They had no power. Only the true God—the Creator of heaven and earth, was worthy to receive honor.

In verses 33-35, David recognizes that it is God who gives him the strength and skill to fight in battles. He likens his feet like those of a deer who can effortlessly scale the heights.

The Old Testament prophet Habakkuk also acknowledged this when he wrote in 3:19, "The Sovereign LORD is my strength; he makes my feet like the feet of a deer, he enables me to go on the heights."

David understood that victory is given by God alone. *He* is the One who fights for us and brings triumph! The last line says it all…" You stoop down to make me great." God, in His infinite wisdom and mercy, chooses those He exalts. God had taken David from a humble shepherd boy out in the field, to king over Israel. Only the Lord could do that. Only God can lift you up and take you to places unseen or unimagined. Only He can win the victory.

HOW DO YOU FACE YOUR GREATEST BATTLES? DO YOU RELY ON A WHIMSICAL LUCK OR DO YOU TRUST IN THE GOD WHO CREATED ALL THINGS AND HOLDS YOU IN THE PALM OF HIS HAND?

DAY 19

PSALM 19:1-6

"The heavens declare the glory of God; the skies proclaim the work of his hands. Day after day they pour forth speech; night after night they display knowledge. There is no speech or language where their voice is not heard. Their voice goes out into all the earth, their words to the ends of the world. In the heavens he has pitched a tent for the sun, which is like a bridegroom coming forth from his pavilion, like a champion rejoicing to run his course. It rises at one end of the heavens and makes its circuit to the other; nothing is hidden from its heat."

~*~

[David is describing the glory of God using the heavens and all their wonderment to showcase His awesome hand of creation.]

As a little girl, I loved stargazing. Often in the late evening, my dad and I would go outside and look up. Dad would point out the Big Dipper and the North Star, the Milky Way, and other constellation groupings. I was always amazed by God's handiwork, especially when the realization hit that I was a dust speck in comparison to the vastness of the universe, yet God knew me intimately. Humbling, to say the least.

Here, David is rejoicing over the clearly seen evidence of God's creation. He looked at the vast sky—the sunrise of the morning and the colors of the sunset at night. The stars in all their glory and the moon shining forth its light. All of this glorious universe cried out the name of its Creator!

David describes these majestic elements as pouring forth speech. They are like a gushing water, revealing God's creativeness, His majesty, and His grandeur. It is said that if the sky were void of the brilliance of God's handiwork, the darkness would proclaim that there is no one out there. Yet, in His great love, He has set them all in place one by one. Each galaxy, star, planet, etc., gives glory back to their Maker; they sing His name!

So, before you begin your day or rest your head tonight, look around and up and see God's creation. He gave it all to us for our pleasure, but also for His glory. Thank Him for these magnificent treasures!

HOW DOES GOD SPEAK TO YOU WHEN YOU LOOK AT THE STARS AT NIGHT?

DAY 20

"Some trust in chariots and some in horses, but we trust in the name of the Lord our God. They are brought to their knees and fall, but we rise up and stand firm."

~*~

[A psalm of David, but perhaps a prayer by the people on David's behalf.]

My mom was probably my greatest prayer warrior. She prayed over and for me from the time I was conceived until her dying breath, and I know her prayers moved God's heart on my behalf.

In this psalm, the people are lifting up their voices on David's account. They and David recognize the fact that some kings put *their* trust in the power of their army. Nations all throughout history have done the same thing; people naturally feel more secure when they possess the greater arsenal. Yet, this was not the plan David had in place, and not simply by choice, but because God had instructed it.

In Deuteronomy 17:16, in God's instructions to the Israelites before entering the Promised Land, He had commanded the future king not to acquire great numbers of horses for himself. Why? The king and nation would fall into the same old pattern of looking to their own limited strength and not to God.

Instead, we read here in this psalm that David's trust would come in the name of the LORD. And where does that get them? David and his army stood secure even after the others had been defeated. God's name is powerful. His name is above all names. He is ready to step in and save.

When we find ourselves in situations where we're tempted to rely on our 401k, a particular leader, or to a certain method, we should choose to turn to God, instead. Only He has infinite power and every answer.

DO YOU FIND IT IS EASY TO PUT YOUR TRUST IN GOD OVER OTHER THINGS? CONTEMPLATE WHY OR WHY NOT.

DAY 21

"Your hand will lay hold on all your enemies; your right hand will seize your foes. At the time of your appearing, you will make them like a fiery furnace. In his wrath the LORD will swallow them up, and his fire will consume them. You will destroy their descendants from the earth, their posterity from mankind. Though they plot evil against you and devise wicked schemes, they cannot succeed; for you will make them turn their backs when you aim at them with drawn bow."

~*~

[A psalm of David, thanking God for the victory that he had been given from his enemies, and the victory God would ultimately have against *all* enemies.]

This is a hard passage. No one likes to think about a time of accountability, but God's Word does not shy away from it, and neither should we. David is not only reflecting on how God will deal with David's current enemies, but this passage is a nod at what is to come in the future.

There will come a day when God declares an end to the wickedness on earth. Those who get away with their evil deeds now, later will have to pay the price of what they have sown. We also know from other verses throughout the Bible that "evil" men don't refer solely to a person's deeds, but also to anyone who rejects God in this lifetime.

Jesus warned people often about a place where the fires never die out, and people are separated from God's great mercy and love. It makes one shudder to think of that eternal agony. Yet, it is a real place, and one too many have chosen to enter because of their sinful, stubborn, prideful hearts. They've rejected God in this life, have gone their own way, lived their own life, and failed to accept the gift of salvation that Jesus offered time and again.

There is coming a day when God will judge the earth. It is my prayer that you have made yourself ready by desperately grasping on to His gift of salvation and being covered by His holy righteousness. **HAVE YOU EXPERIENCED THAT HEART TRANSFORMATION ONLY GOD CAN BRING? IF SO, HOW CAN THAT CHANGE IN YOU HELP OTHERS?**

DAY 22

PSALM 22:27-28

"All the ends of the earth will remember and turn to the LORD, and all the families of the nations will bow down before him, for dominion belongs to the LORD and he rules over the nations."

~*~

[This passage comes towards the end of an entire chapter which devotes itself not only to David's current hardships, but the then future sufferings of Christ on the cross.]

I like a good point. If I'm going to have to go through a tough season, a heavenly test, or a physical ailment, I would like to know the point behind it. Experiencing a hardship for nothing is extremely taxing.

As Jesus hung dying on the cross, He understood the horrors of torture. He embraced the weight of the world's sins, yet even then, He looked forward to the "fruit" His suffering would bear.

Jesus knew that His death would make waves around the world. That is why He came. People—all of us—is why He died. Because of His great love, His death would mean life to those who embraced Him. Many would abandon their sinful ways and turn to Him.

Hebrews 12:2b says, "…who for the joy set before him endured the cross, scorning its shame, and sat down at the right hand of the throne of God."

Jesus was able to look past the pain and shame, and focus on the prize that awaited Him—His people being rescued from the chains that bound them. Ultimately, there was a reason Jesus suffered, died and rose again from the dead; Jesus has bound the "wages of sin" and now points us to the salvation He freely paid for and offers to all of us.

DOES IT HELP TO KNOW THERE IS A REASON BEHIND THE DIFFICULTIES GOD ALLOWS IN YOUR LIFE? HAVE YOU MADE PEACE WITH THE FACT THAT YOU MAY NEVER KNOW THIS SIDE OF HEAVEN SOME OF THOSE REASONS? WHY NOT ASK GOD TO HELP YOU FEEL HIS PEACE AND CONTENTMENT IN THIS SEASON OF WAITING.

DAY 23

"The Lord is my shepherd, I shall not be in want. He makes me lie down in green pastures, he leads me beside quiet waters, he restores my soul. He guides me in paths of righteousness for his name's sake. Even though I walk through the valley of the shadow of death, I will fear no evil, for you are with me; your rod and your staff, they comfort me. You prepare a table before me in the presence of my enemies. You anoint my head with oil; my cup overflows. Surely goodness and love will follow me all the days of my life, and I will dwell in the house of the LORD forever."

~*~

[A psalm of David celebrating God as the great Shepherd-King.]

This is probably one of the most repeated passages in Scripture. David likens himself to a sheep being cared for by the Great Shepherd.

In verse one, he notes a personal relationship with the Lord, as he refers to God as *my* Shepherd. And, because of this special bond, David lacks nothing, for God has supplied all his needs. The Lord sees to it that

David finds quiet rest from the busyness and burdens of life. It is in these moments that the Lord restores and guides him.

Philip Keller, in his book, *A Shepherd Looks at Psalm 23*, writes, "sheep do not lie down easily and will not unless four conditions are met. Because they are timid, they will not lie down if they are afraid. Because they are social animals they will not lie down if there is friction among the sheep. If flies or parasites trouble them, they will not lie down. Finally, if sheep are anxious about food or hungry, they will not lie down. Rest comes because the shepherd has dealt with fear, friction, flies, and famine."[2]

In verse four, David recognizes the fact that though he will face trouble, and possibly even death, he doesn't have to be afraid, for God is right beside him protecting and comforting. [A shepherd's staff was used to pull the sheep back to the shepherd's side; to fight off predators that might want to harm the sheep; and also used to turn the sheep this way or that.]

Also, the fact that David uses the term "shadow" points to his understanding that God would limit the sting of darkness. He would only face a shadow of what was to come, as the Shepherd-King (Jesus) would bear the entire brunt, including death. Fear must flee where the King's presence resides. His light cannot be snuffed out.

---

[2] "Psalm 23-The Lord is My Shepherd and My Host," David Guzik, https://enduringword.com/bible-commentary/psalm-23/.

Verse five displays the Shepherd-King inviting David, even in the presence of his enemies, to a great banquet of honor where he is anointed and his cup kept full, but it also reflects one who cares for his sheep clearing out an area for them to graze while keeping watch.

Finally, in verse six, David recognizes that because the Great Shepherd is with him, he will not stray, but will dwell with Him forever; the two "angels," mercy and goodness, never leaving his side. The Lord has made a covenant with David forever.

THIS is our God!

HOW HAS THE GOOD SHEPHERD LED AND CARED FOR YOU LATELY?

DAY 24

"The earth is the LORD's, and everything in it, the world, and all who live in it; for he founded it on the seas and established it upon the waters. Who may ascend the hill of the LORD? Who may stand in his holy place? He who has clean hands and a pure heart, who does not lift up his soul to an idol or swear by what is false."

~*~

[A psalm of celebration, possibly composed when the ark was brought to Jerusalem, or for remembrance of that special occasion.]

As a child, I remember we always had supper at 4:00 PM sharp. Everyone would gather around the table, but not before we'd all washed our hands. It was unthinkable even to come near mom's kitchen if our hands were not scrubbed clean. There were expectations, and if those expectations were not met, we were sent right back down the hallway to clean up.

Here, David is celebrating the Lord's Kingdom, and it is thought he was writing this when the ark of the covenant was being brought into the place prepared for it.

In verses one and two, we see that everything and everyone belongs to the Lord! HE is Creator God. HE formed the earth and the galaxies. HE set everything in motion. HE measured out the universe precisely without defect. HE brought forth life, and HE revealed Himself to mankind so we might have a relationship with Him. We are mere tenants of a world that belongs solely to Him.

Who then, who can come into the Lord's presence? Surely, He is too mighty and powerful for mere man to enter even into His shadow! No, the Lord opens the door of fellowship to those who have clean hands and a pure heart. Those who have considered their ways and have realized that they are a sinful creature in need of a healing touch of a mighty Savior! Those who put the Lord God first and who lay aside all other idols in their life.

Jesus says, "Come and dine!" Yes! You and I can have access to the very throne room of God if we have Christ's righteousness as our covering. Praise Him!

HOW CAN YOU HAVE CLEAN HANDS AND A PURE HEART IN TODAY'S SOCIETY?

DAY 25

PSALM 25:4-5

"Show me your ways, O LORD, teach me your paths; guide me in your truth and teach me, for you are God my Savior, and my hope is in you all day long."

~*~

[David is praying to God for His covenant mercies and deliverance from evil men. It was David's belief that if God would relieve him of his afflictions, then his enemies would have nothing left to use against him.]

In Chapter 25, David is reflecting on many aspects of his life. These words, perhaps, were written in later years as he pleaded with God in verse seven, "Remember not the sins of my youth and my rebellious ways..."

Yet here in verses four and five, we see David's tender heart seeking to do what pleases the Lord. "Show me your ways...teach me your paths...guide me in your truth." These are words we should desire to say to God each day, for they display wisdom, humility, and a heart that is set on Him.

Finally, David again acknowledges that God alone

is His Savior, and his hope resides in God and who He is. In these uncertain times, where does your hope lie?

Today, on this new day from the Lord, let us humbly petition and ask Him to show, teach, and guide us. May we rest in God's great sovereignty knowing our hope comes from Him and not from anything or anyone else!

WHAT ARE SOME THINGS GOD IS TEACHING YOU IN THIS SEASON OF LIFE?

DAY 26

"Test me, O LORD, and try me, examine my heart and my mind; for your love is ever before me, and I walk continually in your truth."

~*~

[This psalm is David's prayer for vindication, and for God to examine David's heart and bestow His heavenly mercies upon him.]

I remember as a child when my sister would accidentally break something, and mom would be ready to put the hammer down on one or both of us. If I was the innocent one (which was rare), I would be quick to say, "It wasn't me!"

That is sort of what was going on here. David knew he was innocent of all the misdeeds of the ungodly. In this chapter, David is pleading with God to see his heart; to remember all the times he has lived uprightly and honored his Lord. This servant-king asks God to test, try, and examine his ways, and is confident that God will find a heart full of unwavering love.

David was not perfect as we've discussed before. He was a sinner just like everyone else, yet, while he sometimes deviated from the path, the overall direction he travelled was towards God. He was rightfully dubbed, "A man after God's own heart."

Our walk with Christ is about direction, not perfection. We may sometimes make wrong choices and take detours we shouldn't, but if we have made Jesus Lord of our life, then our overall direction should move towards Him!

DOES YOUR DIRECTION POINT TOWARDS JESUS? IF NOT, WHY NOT?

DAY 27

PSALM 27:1

"The LORD is my light and my salvation— whom shall I fear? The LORD is the stronghold of my life— of whom shall I be afraid?"

~*~

[A psalm of David possibly written when he was being pursued by his enemies or perhaps written at the deaths of his parents, whatever the occasion, David found His trust in the Lord.]

As a kid at camp, I remember a group of us walking through the woods one night. At one point, the flashlights went off, and we began to squeal with delight and terror at the sounds of rustling leaves, an occasional hoot from an owl, and the gurgle of the flowing creek. It was deafening. Yet, as soon as the light came back on, we once again felt safe and sure-footed.

In this beginning verse, David refers to the Lord as his "light." David's subjects often called David "the light of Israel" (2 Samuel 21:17), yet David realized that any light in him came from spending time in God's presence.

What is a light's purpose? It is there to illuminate and guide, and because God is our light, He shows us the way so that we do not aimlessly wander.

David also refers to the Lord as his stronghold. What is a stronghold? It is a place of fortification…of security and survival. David understood that God provided him these things, and we, too, can have security and assurance when we place our trust in Him.

God is our Great Defender, and He will fight all our battles. There is an account in the Old Testament about three, young, Hebrew men who were bound and thrown into a fiery furnace because of their refusal to bow down to an idol. When the king looked inside, he saw not three but four men walking around, unbound, and untouched by the flames! This reminds us that though we may walk through the fire, because God is our light and stronghold, we will not be consumed. The Lord will be there right beside us!

TODAY, ASK GOD TO ILLUMINATE YOUR PATH. PETITION HIM TO HELP YOU TO NOT BE ANXIOUS ABOUT LIFE'S CIRCUMSTANCES, RATHER, TO GIVE YOU A SENSE OF HIS PRESENCE IN THE MIDST OF IT ALL. HE WILL ANSWER. HE'S ALREADY THERE.

DAY 28

"The Lord is my strength and my shield; my heart trusts in him, and I am helped. My heart leaps for joy, and I will give thanks to him in song."

~*~

[A psalm of David for deliverance from those evil ones who have pursued him and done much harm. David ends the psalm with praise for what he knows the Lord is going to do.]

There is a meme I've seen circling social media which shows a mom and a child hunkered on the ground as the woman holds up her arm with an invisible shield covering them; the devil's fiery darts bounce off the shield. The point is to display how important a parent's love and prayers are for his or her children. Because of a parent's intercession and God's mighty shield of protection, our children are not consumed by the enemy's advances.

In this verse, David is praising God for being his source of help and strength. He likens God to a shield which deflects all the fiery arrows hurled against him.

David trusts God to step in and help when

troubled times surround, and he is filled with joy to see God in action on his behalf. David delights in his relationship with God, for who is there besides the Mighty One?

So, this recalls the question: do you and I delight in God? Do we praise Him for all the times He has stepped in and fought our battles? Do we acknowledge the many ways He saves us and provides?

When we walk through the trials of life, He is there. When we fail to give Him credit for our success, He is still there. God deserves our praise. May we display our thankfulness to Him today.

RECALL TWO OR THREE BLESSINGS YOU'VE RECEIVED RECENTLY AND GIVE THANKS FOR THEM, EVEN IF YOU'VE GIVEN THANKS FOR THEM IN THE PAST.

DAY 29

"Ascribe to the LORD the glory due his name; worship the LORD in the splendor of his holiness."

~*~

[A psalm of David penned perhaps during a great thunderstorm, to show God's majesty and power.]

Have you ever lain in bed at night during a storm and listened to thunder boom, watched as the flashes of lightning danced across the room? It can be a little unnerving, especially when it the rain is accompanied by strong winds. Yet, it reminds you and me Who God is. He is the maker of heaven and earth, and, just as God asked the prophet Job, "Do you send the lightning bolts on their way? Do they report to you, 'Here we are'?" we need those daily reminders. Often, we forget about God's power over creation, but knowing that He even orders the lightning, helps us to reflect on His majesty.

In Psalm 29:2, David is calling on us to realize our need to give God glory always, for He alone is worthy. When we grumble and complain; stew and fret or just get full of ourselves, we rob God of the glory that is His.

David—an earthly king—recognized that no wealth he could acquire, no pomp or splendor in earthly courts could measure up to God's majesty in His heavenly throne room.

Today, let us not forget to remember Who has placed the sun into the sky; Who it is Who holds the world in balance; and Who has created each of us to enjoy all He has provided. Let us give Him glory, for He is our Eternal King!

TAKE A MOMENT TO THINK OF ALL THE WAYS IN WHICH GOD HAS BEEN GOOD TO YOU?

DAY 30

*"Sing to the LORD, you saints of his; praise his holy name.
For his anger lasts only a moment, but his favor lasts a
lifetime; weeping may remain for a night, but rejoicing
comes in the morning."*

~*~

**[A psalm of David for God's deliverance which
may have been penned after a serious illness or upon
the dedication of the House of David.]**
Have you ever felt as if God was mad at you?
Perhaps you sinned in some way and it seemed as if
He'd completely turned His back. Listen, friend,
though God is grieved when we sin, He always
continues to pursue us as He waits for our return. We
may have consequences to endure because of what
we've done, but when we repent, God is always quick
to forgive, and to restore us to a right relationship with
Him.

In this verse, David is rejoicing in the fact that God
is holy. He is morally perfect and right. In Him there is
no sin or wrongdoing, and His leading and work is
always perfect.

David reminds us that when we turn from God, as when Israel turned away, God's anger is aroused. Just as a parent is disheartened at a child's disobedience, God must supply consequences to our sin so we may learn how detrimental that sinful action is to us and others, and so we may come to abhor our sin as much as He does.

The good news, however, is that once we repent (recognize our wrongful action, turn from it and ask for forgiveness), God restores us with joy! Like a loving Daddy, the punishment is over and now we can continue to rest in His arms of love and protection.

TODAY, IF THERE IS ANYTHING STANDING BETWEEN YOU AND GOD, ACKNOWLEDGE THAT TO HIM, THEN BE RESTORED. WEEPING MAY LAST FOR A NIGHT, BUT JOY COMES IN THE MORNING!

DAY 31

PSALM 31:4-5

"Free me free from the trap that is set for me, for you are my refuge. Into your hands I commit my spirit; redeem me, O LORD, the God of truth."
Psalms 31:4-5

~*~

[This psalm was David's prayer for deliverance when his enemies were advancing upon him.]

Have you ever been in a situation where someone tried to trap you, perhaps with words you said or didn't say, or action you took or failed to take? It is quite possible that they blamed you at work for something you did not do or were trying to make sure you failed as a leader. These times can be overwhelmingly hurtful, and David was no stranger to the pain.

Saul was David's biggest enemy, and in his fits of rage and jealousy, he sought David out to kill him. Yet, David was reminded that he had the advantage. God was his refuge and nothing or no one could snatch David out of God's hand.

In Chapter 31, the shepherd-king is writing a

prayer of deliverance from those who are trying to ensnare him. In verse 4, his enemies have set a trap [for him] and David is petitioning God to keep him from falling for or into it.

We, too, have traps set all around us: those of temptation, a lack of contentment, feelings of hatred, jealousy, covetousness, unforgiveness, and pride. We must seek the Lord's help to maneuver through them or else we will fall and be consumed.

In verse 5, David prophetically pens the words of Christ when he says, "Into your hands I commit my Spirit." Just as Christ gave His very life in obedience to His Father's will, so we should give our lives as a living sacrifice, going, doing, being, whatever He calls us to.

WHAT ATTITUDES, EMOTIONS, OR SITUATIONS ARE ENTRAPPING YOU? ASK GOD TO SET YOU FREE!

DAY 32

"Blessed is he whose transgressions are forgiven, whose sins are covered. Blessed is the man whose sin the LORD does not count against him and in whose spirit is no deceit. When I kept silent, my bones wasted away through my groaning all day long. For day and night your hand was heavy on me; my strength was sapped as in the heat of summer. Then I acknowledged my sin to you and did not cover up my iniquity. I said, 'I will confess my transgressions to the LORD.' And you forgave the guilt of my sin."

~*~

[This psalm is a testimony of David regarding God's gift of forgiveness to those who have sinned against Him, yet who have confessed.]

David was no stranger to sin. He had slept with another man's wife and had the man killed at the front lines of war. Whether he was writing about that season of waywardness or something else, he demonstrates the heaviness of his sins and how they caused him to decline in health.

Yet, when David finally confessed those things over to God, it was as if a great weight had lifted from his shoulders. God forgave David and restored his joy and peace.

When you and I come to the point of surrender, when we lay down our sins before the Lord, He is faithful to forgive us. There is no greater joy but to know we have been forgiven and set free from the burdens we carried for so long. Today is the day. That baggage you are carrying is too heavy. Lay it down, friend.

CONTEMPLATE A TIME WHEN YOUR SIN FELT COMPLETELY OVERWHELMING AND RECONSIDER HOW YOU FELT WHEN YOU ASKED FOR AND RECEIVED FORGIVENESS. IF NOW IS A TIME YOU'RE OVERWHELMED BY SIN, HAND THEM OVER TO THE LORD AND ASK FOR FORGIVENESS. WHEN YOU SINCERELY ASK TO BE FORGIVEN, GOD'S ANSWER IS ALWAYS, "YES", SO YOU HAVE NOTHING TO LOSE!

DAY 33

PSALM 33:10-11

"The LORD foils the plans of the nations; he thwarts the purposes of the peoples. But the plans of the LORD stand firm forever, the purposes of his heart through all generations."."

~*~

[No author is mentioned, but it is possible that David penned it. The psalmist calls the righteous to praise God for His justice, goodness, sovereignty, His work in creation, truth, and His favor.]

In 1933, Adolf Hitler was appointed chancellor of Germany, and from that time on, made it his mission to dominate as world power, and to purge Germany of what he considered to be the insufficient races by exterminating some six million Jews, Catholics and sympathizers. Hitler, however, did not have the final say. In April of 1945, while hunkered down in a Berlin bunker stewing over news of Germany's losing hand in the Battle of Berlin, Hitler took his own life. Though this man was able to do much damage, ultimately, God foiled his plans. Hitler's wickedness caught up to him.

Oh, how humans like to think they are in charge!

National leaders with their lofty plans hold nothing to the power of God. He overrules their schemes and uses their wicked intentions to carry out His ultimate, and perfect, plan.

Evil people come and go, but God and His will stand forever. Though situations may look bleak, times may be challenging, do not forget *Who* is still in charge of His creation! God cannot be undone, nor His authority stripped. He has the final say.

The psalmist goes on to write, "From heaven the LORD looks down and sees all mankind; from his dwelling places he watches all who live on earth—he who forms the hearts of all, who considers everything they do. (vs. 13-15)"

God sees. Nothing escapes the eye of the Lord, and there will come a day when man has to give an account. As for you and me, today let us consider our ways and stand on the side of the Lord.

HOW DO YOU SEE GOD MOVING IN THE POLITICAL TIMES OF OUR WORLD TODAY? IF TIMES SEEM BLEAK OR GODLESS, CONSIDER THE FACT THAT YOU ARE READING THIS BOOK, WHICH GOD ALLOWED TO BE PUBLISHED!

DAY 34

PSALM 34:7-10

"The angel of the LORD encamps around those who fear him, and he delivers them. Taste and see that the LORD is good; blessed is the man who takes refuge in him. Fear the Lord, you his saints, for those who fear him lack nothing. The lions may grow weak and hungry, but those who seek the LORD lack no good thing."

~*~

[A psalm of God's deliverance of David when David became like a madman before Abimelech.]

In this passage, David is giving God praise for sparing his life from a Philistine king, but, also, he is encouraging others to turn to the Lord.

First, in verse seven we see that God sends angels to surround those who "fear" Him. The type of fear David is describing here means to revere, honor, respect, and to obey the Lord. These angels offer deliverance and protection, but they also console and encourage us in our moments of weakness.

Second, David offers us a challenge: Go ahead! Check out God for yourself. You'll never know His goodness or the blessings which come with a relationship with Him unless you first *taste and see.*

Third, we are called to fear God. Not to be scared as we would be of the dark or some other ominous entity, but rather to have a sense of awe and holy trembling of His great majesty and power. David reminds us that if we do these things, we will not lack any good thing because God enjoys supplying the needs of His children, and though we will not receive an answer to every whim or fascination, He will see that our imminent needs are met.

Finally, David says, "the lions may grow weak and hungry, but those who seek the LORD lack no good thing." Those mighty ones (mighty in their own eyes) will eventually be empty handed. Nothing will satisfy their hunger. However, individuals who feast on the Lord (fix their eyes, serve Him continually) will be satisfied. God never leaves a person with less than they had before. No, when we come into a relationship with Him, we have a life richly abundant with satisfaction in Him.

RECALL WAYS IN WHICH GOD HAS BEEN GOOD TO YOU. HAVE YOU SEEN HIS HAND OF DIRECTION AND PROTECTION UPON YOUR LIFE?

DAY 35

"My tongue will speak of your righteousness, and of your praises all day long."

~*~

[David is petitioning the Lord to come to his aid. Individuals who were once friends have turned against him, and he is in distress.]

Have you ever been around someone who has literally lost everything, perhaps to violence, natural disaster, or some other incident, yet they continue to give glory to God? I hate to say it, but it is rare. Most people want to blame God for their misfortunes, yet every now and then, you might run across someone who, despite their circumstances, is able to declare that God is still good.

In Chapter 35, David is bemoaning the fact that even though he has treated his enemies with integrity and generosity, they are seeking to take his life and bring shame.

Sometimes in life, we can do all the right things, say all the kind words, and yet a person will continue to attack our character. This can cause us to become weary and frustrated with the circumstances and to question why.

Yet, in David's situation, he ends his psalm with a final resolve—but I'm *still* going to give You praise, God. He's in a difficult situation, but his focus remains on the Lord. He doesn't know how it will end, but he knows God is able to resolve it, and that God's resolution will be perfect.

Do you and I have that same faith? Do we say, "Well, this situation is not good and I don't like it, but I'm going to praise God while I'm waiting for answers?" I hope we can come to that point of faith.

If you are struggling today with something or someone, hand it over to God then walk away praising Him. It will change your whole outlook.

HOW ARE YOU GIVING GOD PRAISE IN THE MIDST OF YOUR DIFFICULTIES?

DAY 36

PSALM 36:5-9

"Your love, O LORD, reaches to the heavens, your faithfulness to the skies. Your righteousness is like the mighty mountains, your justice like the great deep. O LORD, you preserve both man and beast. How priceless is your unfailing love! Both high and low among men find refuge in the shadow of your wings. They feast on the abundance of your house; you give them drink from your river of delights. For with you is the fountain of life; in your light we see light."

~*~

[A song of David regarding the godlessness of the wicked, God's great protection, and His goodness towards those who follow Him.]

Turn on the news and you may be soon overwhelmed by all the evil. Sometimes it can seem as if the enemy has the upper hand, and you and I can become anxious and even frightened by all that is taking place in our world. However, this Psalm verse reminds us,that even though there are many individuals who love darkness rather than light, God's eye is on the righteous, and His love and faithfulness cannot be undone.

David compares and contrasts the wicked who have no fear of God, with the righteous who find refuge in the shadow of God's wings.

He paints a picture of God's immeasurable qualities. His love is higher than the heavens; His righteousness stands tall and unmovable like the mightiest mountains; His justice vaster than the depths of the sea.

David praises God for not only providing and preserving human life, but the animal kingdom as well. God's love for His creation is unfailing! And because of God's mercy and generosity towards us, we have abundance in Him, and He delights us with all He has to offer. God is our eternal light, and if we walk with Him, we will not stumble because He will illuminate our path.

We have *much* to be thankful for on this morning and every morning! Praise the Lord!

WHAT IS ONE WAY YOU CAN REFOCUS ON GOD AND HIS GOODNESS TODAY?

DAY 37

"Be still before the LORD and wait patiently for him..."
Psalms 37:7

~*~

[A teaching psalm that evaluates the prosperity of the wicked and the hardships of the righteous.]

It is hard to wait, especially when we are waiting on justice to be served. In certain circumstances, we may never receive answers, or what we think is due punishment for wrong done to us, but that is not our concern. While the wait for justice is difficult, vengeance belongs to the Lord, and we can rest assured that He is faithful to reward those who have walked faithfully with Him, and to sentence those justly who have harbored wickedness in their heart without repentance.

Chapter 37 is all about the wicked receiving what is due, and God rewarding those with "the land" or an inheritance, who have followed fast after Him.

Verse 7a sums up the entire chapter: wait patiently on God. When it seems as if wicked men have the upper hand, wait on God. When our prayers seem unanswered, wait on God. He will vindicate. He will have the last word. God is in control, and He works in His timing. Yet, His timing may not be ours, so we simply must seek Him, lay out our petitions, then trust He will answer.

There is coming a day when those who have continually come against God and His people will receive their dues. Likewise, those who have been faithful will receive eternal blessing and peace.

So, I encourage you, be still, be patient, and wait for the Lord.

WHAT THINGS DO YOU DO TO HELP YOU WAIT ON GOD?

DAY 38

PSALM 38:18

"I confess my iniquity; I am troubled by my sin."

~*~

[David is experiencing both illness and loss. Due to sinful choices, God has given him over to illness, but with it, his friends have all pulled away.]

Are we troubled by our sin? Have you ever turned away from God in a moment of weakness, only to experience stronger feelings of emptiness, helplessness, and loneliness?

In Chapter 38, David is struggling with a sense that God is disciplining him, and he feels abandoned. Sin is troubling his spirit.

The first step to reconciliation with God is to recognize and acknowledge our sin. We must go to Him with our troubled heart and ask with sincerity for forgiveness.

David realized that he was far from God, and because his heart was still tender, he understood that the only place that mattered was on his knees, and the only person who mattered was his Savior.

IS YOUR SIN TROUBLING YOU? WHAT STEPS DID YOU

TAKE TO CORRECT IT?

DAY 39

"You have made my days a mere handbreadth; the span of my years is as nothing before you. Each man's life is but a breath."

~*~

[A prayer of anguish by David, who was deeply troubled over the brevity of life. In his own sickness and frailties, he recognized that first, he was a sinful man, and second, he should be patient and wait on God to move on his behalf.]

If you have ever attended the funeral of someone whose life was cut short seemingly well before their time, you understand the words of David. Life comes and goes so quickly. In light of eternity, even a long lifespan is nothing but a mist, here one moment and gone the next.

David recognized the fact that his life was a vapor compared to God's eternity. This should make us stop and think about how futile it is to store up treasures here on earth when in the grand scheme of things, we are only here just a little while.

David goes on to say that everyone rushes about

heaping up "wealth not knowing who will get it. (vs. 6b)" What he is talking about here are the things to which we become enslaved—our jobs, fancy homes, clothes, the latest gadgets, etc. One day, they will all belong to someone else or will be thrown into a trash heap. David recognizes that hope should not be put in those things, but in God (vs. 7).

Where is your focus? Do you find yourself wrapped up in gaining wealth or friends or in performing well in the eyes of man, or are you placing your Hope and security in Christ?

DAY 40

"I waited patiently for the LORD; he turned to me and heard my cry. He lifted me out of the slimy pit, out of the mud and mire; he set my feet on a rock and gave me a firm place to stand. He put a new song in my mouth, a hymn of praise to our God. Many will see and fear and put their trust in the LORD."

~*~

[David is again wrestling with his sin and predicaments in life. He knows that God is His only hope and so, he turns to Him for help.]

Can you think of a time when God helped you out of a low place? Perhaps something had caused you to spiral downward, or maybe you had run away from God so as not to have to do what He was asking of you.

David was experiencing this first-hand. He was in a place of despair, yet God was gracious, and after some time, placed David in a new place of service. In verses 1-3, David reflects back on the things God has done in his life. Since we so often get caught up in our present-day frustrations and stresses, and simply forget, it is good for us to remember the Lord's goodness.

Think of those moments God stepped in and delivered a seemingly impossible outcome or provided help or financial assistance from an unexpected person or place. Or, what about the blessings He has brought to you through, our family, our job, our ministry? There is certainly a lot to be thankful for. God is so good.

When times become difficult, reflect back and see the hand of God's blessing. He didn't fail you then and He won't fail you moving forward. That is His promise to us.

MAKE NOTE OF HOW GOD HAS PULLED YOU OUT OF A LOW PLACE AND GIVEN YOU A NEW DIRECTION.

DAY 41

"Blessed is he who has regard for the weak; the LORD delivers him in times of trouble."

~*~

[David was extremely ill and in dire need of God's help. His illness wasn't from physical disease, but rather from his spiritual sin (vs. 4)., and only the Great Physician could heal him.]

In Chapter 41, During a time of distress, David is expressing his thoughts about those who do good to him, and those who bring him even more suffering. In verse one, he is either talking about his loyal servants and friends or is referring to the actions he has taken towards others in the past. Possibly both.

David calls "blessed" those who have regard or look after others who are weaker. You and I often come across people who are not as strong physically, emotionally, spiritually, etc. If we treat them with respect as a person made in God's image, instead of with callousness, harshness, or disdain, then, David says, God will have mercy and deliver us in times of our own trouble. Of course, this doesn't mean we will not struggle in this life, even if we treat others with kindness, but God will walk through those struggles with us and give us aid such as we have given to those around us when they were in need.

Jesus said, "Give, and it will be given to you...For with the measure you use, it will be measured to you." Luke 6:38

HOW HAS GOD ENABLED YOU LATELY TO MINISTER TO SOMEONE WHO IS HURTING OR STRUGGLING WITH SOMETHING?

DAY 42

"As the deer pants for streams of water, so my soul pants for you, O God. My soul thirsts for God, for the living God. When can I go and meet with God?"

~*~

[Written from the pen of one afflicted, yet understanding God's immeasurable grace, this song was composed for the Sons of Korah to sing and show their gratitude for what God had done for them.]

One hot summer afternoon, my husband and I went for what we thought was a short hike. Because we weren't going to be gone long, we did not take water...first mistake. Due to our unfamiliarity with the trail and because we lost sight of the path, the short hike became an agonizing one as I envisioned a cold, water bottle wetting my lips. Finally, after a couple of hours, we reached a road and eventually a conservation station where they had cold water waiting. Lesson learned. Never go hiking without water, ever.

In this verse, the psalmist is likening his need for

God to a deer with an unquenchable thirst. He was not describing an occasional want, but rather a life-sustaining requirement.

Like the deer, without the required daily sustenance, the writer would grow faint and eventually perish. We should ask ourselves if we recognize that God is our daily mainstay. Do we feast on His Word regularly? Do we drink of His unending well of wisdom and delight? If not, perhaps our spiritual diet is nothing but empty nothingness, leaving us vulnerable to the enemy's attacks.

My prayer is that these small daily devotions are challenging you to pick up the Word and read for yourself the life-giving words of our Lord. Only through Him can we find true life and refreshment for our spiritual thirst.

HOW HAS GOD REFRESHED YOUR SOUL THIS WEEK?

DAY 43

PSALM 43:5

"Why are you downcast, O my soul? Why so disturbed within me? Put your hope in God, for I will yet praise him, my Savior and my God."

~*~

[This psalm and the one prior were most likely written at the same time. Psalm 43 almost describes the psalmist in a spiritual depression-like state of mind. He is downcast, feels rejected, and almost displays a victim mentality, yet he does express hope in his God.]

Just like the depressed state in which the writer of this psalm found himself, Elijah, one of the great prophets of God, also began to doubt God in a moment of weakness.

In 1 Kings 19:14, we read, "...'I have been very zealous for the LORD God Almighty. The Israelites have rejected your covenant, broken down your altars, and put your prophets to death with the sword. I am the only one left, and now they are trying to kill me too.'" Reading the rest of the story, you will find the situation was not nearly as dire as Elijah had thought.

He was not the only one left and God had plans despite Elijah's weakness.

Likewise, the psalmist, here, is questioning his own attitude in the midst of his difficulties. It is as if he is having a conversation with himself, "Why are you acting like this? You know where your hope comes from. God hasn't failed you before."

Sometimes we have to look hard at our own selves, and ask, "Why am I so anxious or bothered by _____." We have to reflect on God's love and mercy in previous situations and realize that He will come through for us once again.

It is our attitude towards our circumstances which make or break us. We can stay downcast and discouraged, or we can place our hope in the Lord and His ability to develop our character through it. The psalmist recognizes this choice and chooses to place his hope in the Lord.

HAVE YOU EVER FELT AS IF YOU WERE THE ONLY ONE EXPERIENCING PAIN? HOW DID GOD RE-ROUTE YOUR THOUGHTS?

DAY 44

PSALM 44:3

"It was not by their sword that they won the land, nor did their arm bring them victory; it was your right hand, your arm, and the light of your face, for you loved them."

~*~

[This psalm is a cry for help after a stunning defeat. However, the psalmist praises God for past victories, and pleads with God for His mercies once again.]

The psalmist is referring to the stories of when God brought the Israelites out of the land of Egypt and into the land flowing with milk and honey, which have been passed down throughout generations,.

Here is a reminder. The people's lives were not spared due to their military prowess or intellectual wit, but rather because of God's mighty provision and His defeat of those who came against them. They did not inherit the land of abundance simply because of their own doing, but because they had faith in a God with a greater purpose and plan.

We can and must muster the same faith today. The blessings we have accumulated, the people we hold dear, the battles which have been won on our behalf, they are not our victories, but rather belong to the Lord. We have no right to claim them as our own. It is only through the great love of our heavenly Father and His mercy towards us that we have been blessed and with such abundance.

So, today, I want to say, "thank you, Lord," for the victories and blessings. Without You, I would be nothing.

WHAT ARE SOME SPECIFIC BLESSINGS THAT YOU WANT TO THANK GOD FOR TODAY?

DAY 45

"In your majesty ride forth victoriously in behalf of truth, humility and righteousness; let your right hand display awesome deeds. Let your sharp arrows pierce the hearts of the king's enemies; let the nations fall beneath your feet. Your throne, O God, will last for ever and ever; a scepter of justice will be the scepter of your kingdom."

~*~

[A psalm describing the future Messiah, Christ, and His bride, the church.]

Many of the paintings or renderings we see of Jesus display soft features and a meek disposition. However, this is not the Jesus we see painted in the Bible.

In this psalm, the writer is describing one who is most likely the Messiah in all His glory returning to claim His bride, the church.

In verses 4-6, the bridegroom is pictured as a mighty warrior leading a victorious procession upon truth, humility, and justice. He hurls arrows which do not miss their target, and He either pierces the heart of man with His love or His vengeance. He needs no help but His own right hand to overthrow His enemies. This warrior cannot and shall not be defeated as He carries the bow and has extremely accurate aim.

Finally, this Messiah will reign supreme over all earthly kingdoms. Only *His* Kingdom will last for eternity. He will judge the nations justly and fairly, and His great mercy and love will lend support to the oppressed.

God is the awesome and mighty King! He is coming back and will establish His throne forever. He is worthy to be praised!

HOW DOES KNOWING CHRIST AS A STRONG, MIGHTY, AND VICTORIOUS KING HELP YOU IN YOUR TIMES OF TROUBLE?

DAY 46

"God is our refuge and strength, an ever-present help in trouble. Therefore, we will not fear, though the earth give way and the mountains fall into the heart of the sea..."

~*~

[This is a psalm of encouragement for times we go through difficulties and trial. Trust in God and give glory for what He will do.]

I remember when our kids were young, I had taken them to a Christmas Eve service by myself. Momma needed some Jesus, and dad was working. So, we piled into the car and headed to church. All I can say is: it was a disaster. The kids acted horribly. I was stressed and frustrated, but a kind older lady came out in the foyer where I was crying in a heap. "It's going to be OK. You'll get through this." Her words of encouragement were all I needed to hear in those moments. In the same way, when life is topsy-turvy, God comes alongside us and whispers, "It is going to be OK."

In this Psalm, we are given such encouragement from the Psalter. We are reminded that God is our refuge. Nothing can compare to His protection, peace, and His comfort! He is our great help when all else has failed us. He gives us strength to endure those things we would normally not be able to endure.

And, even when the world as we know it is falling apart and the enemy is relentlessly attacking our families, our nation, our churches, our health, God is our stability. We can still have joy even in the midst of the uncertainties and pain.

The psalmist follows up these verses with God's words to us, "Be still, and know that I am God (vs. 10)."

He is with us. He has overcome the darkness. Be still, child. He still has the wheel.

HOW HAS GOD BEEN YOUR REFUGE IN TIMES OF DIFFICULTY?

DAY 47

PSALM 47:8

"God reigns over the nations; God is seated on his holy throne."

~*~

[A song of praise sung by the Sons of Korah but thought to have been written by David.]

Can you think of a time you gushed over a celebrity or something they said or did? I recently attended a conference for my business, and the owner/creator of the business was there. People flocked to him as if he were some type of movie star. I hate to admit it, but I, too, had feelings of excitement and even had my picture taken with him, yet I kept reminding myself he is just a man who puts on his pants one leg at a time like everyone else. God, however, well, He is a different story!

It is no great secret that God is seated on His throne and has sovereign rule over His creation. Yet, it is a thought so often ignored within our daily routine. The fact remains, God has always reigned; He is currently reigning; and He will forever reign!

In this chapter's entirety, the psalmist is displaying

his utter joy as this great mystery is once and for all revealed and acknowledged. "Clap your hands, all you nations; shout to God with cries of joy (vs. 1)."

He ends the chapter by painting us a snapshot of when, in those glorious days when every eye shall see and every tongue confess, all the nobles of the nations (vs. 9) will gather and pay homage to the King. It will be then when the covenant promise to Abraham will be fulfilled, and the throngs of Abraham's seed like an infinite galaxy, be gathered together for an eternity of holy moments. Hallelujah! And Amen!

WHAT ARE SOME WORDS YOU WOULD USE TO DESCRIBE GOD?

DAY 48

PSALM 48:10

"Like your name, O God, your praise reaches to the ends of the earth; your right hand is filled with righteousness."

~*~

[A psalm rejoicing in the security of Zion with God as their guide.]

We just recently completed a new house build. After almost two years of product delays and skyrocketing lumber and other material prices, we are finally in, and are continuously giving all praises to God who blessed us with such a beautiful treasure to live in. However, an earthly home is no comparison to the heavenly home we will someday inherit.

In Psalm 48, the writer describes the glory of the city of Jerusalem and how its enemies have had to flee because of God's presence there. It was a time of rejoicing, and the psalmist was celebrating with the people, how God fortified the city of Zion and built up their security. His name was echoed throughout the temple and the land because of the great things He had done.

Just like that scenario, God's name still

reverberates through every corner of the world because there is no other name that holds greater power or esteem.

We know from scripture that the praises of His people and of all creation fill the earth. Job 12:7-9 says, "But ask the animals, and they will teach you,or the birds in the sky, and they will tell you; or speak to the earth, and it will teach you, or let the fish in the sea inform you. Which of all these does not know that the hand of the Lord has done this?." Jesus Himself said in Luke 19:40 that even if the people were silenced, the "stones will cry out." In Psalm 8:2 we read, "From the lips of children and infants you have ordained praise because of your enemies, to silence the foe and the avenger." His name cannot be contained. The joy of His presence in our lives cannot be held back. The enemy cannot silence the praise of God's people. We want the world to know what He has done. Don't you?

GOD HAS MANY DIFFERENT NAMES THROUGHOUT THE BIBLE. WHAT IS YOUR FAVORITE?

DAY 49

PSALM 49:16-20

"Do not be overawed when a man grows rich, when the splendor of his house increases; for he will take nothing with him when he dies, his splendor will not descend with him. Though while he lived he counted himself blessed — and men praise you when you prosper — he will join the generation of his fathers, who will never see the light of life. A man who has riches without understanding is like the beasts that perish."

~*~

[This psalm is a word of instruction to those who tend to put their trust in wealth and in themselves for their security. The psalter understands the foolishness of this. He also encourages those less fortunate, who see the wicked seemingly prosper, their end will come soon enough.]

In this chapter, the writer is beckoning the rich and poor to get serious and listen. Wealth will not buy happiness. It cannot save anyone from the eventual end which is death. It cannot buy a person out of eternity.

In this verse, the psalmist states we are not to look

on the one who has a lot of money with envy, because that person will not take one last cent of it when they depart this life. Though people flaunt their riches and live lavishly now, there will come a day when they will be separated from all their earthly possessions and will return to dust.

This is why Jesus tells us in Matthew 6:20, "But store up for yourselves treasures in heaven, where moth and rust do not destroy, and where thieves do not break in and steal."

Riches in the here-and-now do not mean a thing in the light of eternity. A man can accumulate much wealth but still lose his soul if he fails to realize his need for a Savior.

May we always remember true riches lie in store for those who seek hard after God in this life. For those will inherit the Kingdom.

WHAT RICHES ARE YOU STORING UP? ARE YOU MORE CONCERNED WITH EARTHLY WEALTH OR SPIRITUAL TREASURE?

Day 50

"He who sacrifice thank offerings honors me, and he prepares the way so that I may show him the salvation of God."

~*~

[This is a psalm of reproof and correction. God calls the people of the earth to come and hear His declaration. He then describes the type of acceptable worship and condemns the wicked.]

What is it that God wants from us? According to Psalm 51:17, God is seeking a contrite heart and broken spirit. This means, He desires true repentance, not lip-service; humility not pride; and for us to turn to Him for mercy when we've sinned against Him.

Chapter 50 is a psalm of instruction. God is summoning His creation to hear His declaration and judgment, and is telling the people their endless animal sacrifices in rote repetition mean nothing to Him, for He owns cattle on a thousand hills, and has no need for such.

Instead, what He desires is their faithfulness, and in verse 23, reminds them it is their words of praise they offer which bring blessing and honor. People who have experienced the saving Grace of God through His Son, Jesus, know the path to God's heart. When you and I put Him first in our lives and display a posture of humility and thanks for all He has done, God, in turn, accepts our offering and counts us as righteous.

May we always display a grateful heart for all the Lord has done for us.

WHAT TYPE OF THANK OFFERING ARE YOU GOING TO OFFER UP TO GOD TODAY?

Day 51

"Have mercy on me, O God, according to your unfailing love; according to your great compassion blot out my transgressions. Wash away all my iniquity and cleanse me from my sin."

~*~

[This psalm is David's humble confession and prayer for forgiveness after sinning with Bathsheba, Uriah's wife.]

Have you ever done or said something and immediately known you had done or said the wrong thing? I remember a time when words of prideful disgust towards another tumbled out of my mouth. In an instant, I knew I had sinned and needed forgiveness from God.

In Chapter 51, David, after being confronted by Nathan the prophet regarding David's sin with Bathsheba, begs God for mercy as he bows before Him in humble submission. Yes, there were consequences to David's sin, but God never stopped loving him. You see, God is not some evil dictator who takes pleasure in our misery, but rather, a loving, forgiving God beckoning us to come to Him for restoration. David was not beyond forgiveness, and neither are we.

The message of hope shown in this Psalm is for us all. No one is too far to be reached by the merciful hand of God. Jesus desires that we come back to Him. He paid the ultimate penalty for our sins and has made the way for reconciliation with the Father. So, just come.

HAVE YOU EVER FOUND YOURSELF IN A SITUATION WHERE YOU FELT FAR AWAY FROM GOD? HOW DID YOU FIND YOUR WAY BACK TO HIM? IF YOU HAVEN'T FOUND YOUR WAY BACK YET, CONSIDER PRAYING PSALM 51.

DAY 52

PSALM 52:1-3, 7

"Why do you boast of evil, you mighty man? Why do you boast all day long, you who are a disgrace in the eyes of God? Your tongue plots destruction; it is like a sharpened razor. You who practice deceit. You love evil rather than good, falsehood rather than speaking the truth…Here now is the man who did not make God his stronghold but trusted in his great wealth and grew strong by destroying others!"

~*~

[A contrast and comparison between David and his enemy, Doeg, who had betrayed him.]

Have you ever been betrayed? Betrayal of any kind is never easy to maneuver. Its blows run deep and the wounds are hard to heal.

Chapter 52 is David condemning Doeg, the Edomite who had tattled to King Saul about David's whereabouts, which ultimately caused the deaths of all the priests at Nob. Doeg is guilty of boasting, lying, plotting, and trusting in his own wealth and devices; and David warns the man God will have the final say.

In this world, we, too, will witness wicked men and women plotting and scheming, so far removed from God that they have no idea the destructive path to which their feet are affixed.

You and I may feel as if those individuals have the upper hand in their wickedness but know this: God will have the last word. He will not be mocked for long, and if they do not turn from their evil ways, they will be destroyed.

Lest we forget, here also is the message of grace. David, a man who had also committed willful sins, considered himself an "olive tree flourishing in the house of God (vs. 8)." Why? Because he had found forgiveness and hope in his God. David was a changed man because he did not shut the door to God's immeasurable love and mercy.

Today, we need to remember that great are the sins of man, but greater still is the grace of God.

DO YOU HAVE ANY UNCONFESSED SIN IN YOUR LIFE? WHAT'S HOLDING YOU BACK FROM TAKING IT TO GOD?

DAY 53

PSALM 53:1

"The fool says in his heart, 'There is no God.' They are corrupt, and their ways are vile; there is no one who does good."

~*~

[Closely related to Psalm 14, this psalm of David addresses the depravity of man. We are all sinners and it is by His grace we are saved.]

This is a hard verse at the beginning of a difficult chapter. David is laying down the gauntlet. Mankind is morally bankrupt. Many people give God no thought and even claim that He fails to exist.

The writer declares, "there is no one who does good," and then he repeats the phrase a second time at the end of verse 3. But wait! The Apostle Paul reiterates it once more in Romans 3:12 when he says, "there is no one who does good, not even one."

But what about all the good things we do? We provide for our family, work hard, build up our business, show kindness to others. These are all noble things yet they fail miserably short in the presence of God and His holy standard. The prophet Isaiah wrote,

"All our righteous acts are like filthy rags (Is. 64:6a)" Though we are called to live our lives in such a way that others see Jesus in us, no deed is good enough to earn our way into heaven. There is only One who was and is ever able to be declared good, and that is Jesus. This is the whole reason He was sent to earth as a baby to die on a cross as a man. He died so we may have life. He paid the price which should have been ours to pay.

Let us take time to remember *Who* we are worshipping—the Redeemer of the world; the Holy One; Emmanuel; God with us! HE is good!

HAVE YOU EVER HAD A PERSON TELL YOU THEY WOULD GO TO HEAVEN BECAUSE THEY DID GOOD THINGS? WHAT WAS YOUR RESPONSE?

DAY 54

"Surely God is my help; the LORD is the one who sustains me."

~*~

[A prayer of David for deliverance from his enemies, but also confirmation of God's vindication on David's behalf.]

I can think of times when I have cried out to God for help in a particularly hard moment or season, and can say for certain, God has never failed me. However, when I am pressed and squeezed into tight and difficult situations, I tend to forget all the previous times He has come to my aid, and instead, cry out as one who has no hope.

David knew where his help came from. He was no stranger to difficulties and strife, yet he remained steadfast in his faith in God. This is in part because David never failed to recognize how far he'd fallen and how faithfully God had accepted David's repentance and lifted him back up.

You and I will face difficult seasons when it seems as if everyone and everything is against us, but those moments are when we need to press in a little further and refocus our thoughts to things of Him.

Never once has He failed you or me. Our own poor decisions, or those of others, may have ushered us into a bind, but God has never failed. He has always been there encouraging us along, protecting, directing, comforting, forgiving us when we repent. It is God who is worthy of praise. May we, like David, honor Him and remember He is on our side.

HOW HAS GOD SUSTAINED YOU THIS WEEK?

DAY 55

PSALM 55:12-14

"If an enemy were insulting me, I could endure it; if a foe were raising himself against me, I could hide from him. But it is you, a man like myself, my companion, my close friend, with whom I once enjoyed sweet fellowship as we walked with the throng at the house of God."

~*~

[This song is a prayer of David, for God's help of vindication. A former friend had conspired against David, and he's not sure who he can trust anymore. Yet, David understands that God, alone, is trustworthy, and to Him he would pour out his petitions.]

King David was describing an unbearable situation where someone very close, very dear had turned against him. These verses also seem eerily familiar to the relationship between Jesus and his disciple Judas—the betrayed and the betrayer.

You and I are no strangers to being hurt by those closest to us. Sometimes a good friend or family member will create a situation which causes deep grief and loss. It hurts. It cuts to the core. We think to ourselves how much easier it would be if it were a stranger, but a trusted friend? Someone whom I love? This is almost unbearable.

Yet, we know as with the example of Jesus and Judas, up until the very second Judas left the Lord's side to sell him out for thirty pieces of silver, Jesus was showing kindness and love. He had washed the disciples' feet (including Judas's) and had shared a meal, even though Jesus knew Judas would hand Him over to his enemies.

Like Jesus' example, we are to treat our enemies with kindness. The Apostle Paul wrote in Romans 12:20, "On the contrary: 'If your enemy is hungry, feed him; if he is thirsty, give him something to drink. In doing this, you will heap burning coals on his head.'"

It is a hurtful thing when someone wounds us with words or action, but how we respond says so much about our character and *Who* we serve. Be like Jesus.

WHO NEEDS YOUR KINDNESS AND FORGIVENESS TODAY?

DAY 56

PSALM 56:3

"When I am afraid, I will trust in you."

~*~

[Here we find David's plea for God's help after being captured by the Philistines. The psalmist consoles himself with the knowledge that God will be with him despite the circumstances.]

I learned this verse as a child. My mom recited it over me as she sat by my bedside at night. She probably did not realize it then, but she was building a mighty fortress, an arsenal for me which would serve me well in many situations.

In this passage, David had been seized by the Philistines and was expressing both fear and faith—fear as a grown man, a warrior king, who could not save himself or alter his situation in his own strength, but also faith in his God who had been ever faithful to him in times of trial.

We, too, go through fearful and uncertain times, yet we are to remember the *Who* who holds us in His hand. This is where faith comes in. So, when moments of fear start taking root in our thoughts, we must remember to make room for the Savior. Friend, your boat may be rocking, but we serve the One who masters the sea.

IS THERE A SITUATION THAT IS CAUSING YOU TO FEAR? WHY NOT GIVE THAT OVER TO GOD?

DAY 57

PSALM 57:10

"For great is your love, reaching to the heavens; your faithfulness reaches to the skies."

~*~

[This song, created from the depths of the cave, was David's plea for God's deliverance from Saul. Though the beginning has a dark overtone, the ending displays hope in God above.]

Have you ever experienced a season of darkness? Perhaps you were walking through a debilitating illness, a death of a loved one, or had simply just lost your way. The pain can be overwhelming, causing our anxiety levels to skyrocket.

David cried out to God for help and mercy because he knew only God could save him. He was assured the Lord was not finished and would see His purposes for David's life were fulfilled.

We, too, can praise God for all He has done for us. His love is so great that even the heavens cannot contain it; His faithfulness is immeasurable. God cannot and will not fail you or me, and He will see us through to the completion of His will for our lives on this earth.

So today, rest assured that no one or nothing can touch you other than what God has allowed or willed for the furthering of His purposes, and for the strengthening of your faith. Look up, friend. Great is the Father's love and concern for you.

WHAT WAYS HAS GOD SHOWN HIS LOVE FOR YOU?

DAY 58

PSALM 58:1-2

"Do you rulers indeed speak justly? Do you judge uprightly among men? No, in your heart you devise injustice, and your hands mete out violence on the earth."

~*~

[A prayer of David for God to judge and take action over those in powerful positions and places of judicial authority who were breeding corruption and malice.]

David was accusing Saul and his cronies of wickedness towards David, but also against their own people. The message is clear, these men were bent on doing evil and seemingly had no conscience.

We do not have to look far to see the same kinds of leaders. In roles of leadership all over the world, from the local level on up, there are some who would rather destroy their own communities or country than sacrifice their desires for the betterment of the people.

David goes on with his song including harsh words of vindication. He petitions God to break their teeth, tear out their fangs, make them vanish, blunt their arrows, and cause their deaths. David wasn't messing around.

Though we can sympathize with him and try to understand his frustrations, we should notice that Jesus had a different tone and approach. He said, "But I tell you, love your enemies and pray for those who persecute you (Matt. 5:44)."

The Apostle Paul reminded his readers "Do not take revenge, my dear friends, but leave room for God's wrath, for it is written: 'It is mine to avenge; I will repay,' says the Lord (Rom. 12:19)."

And finally, in 1 Timothy we read, "I urge, then, first of all, that requests, prayers, intercession and thanksgiving be made for everyone— for kings and all those in authority, that we may live peaceful and quiet lives in all godliness and holiness. This is good, and pleases God our Savior (1 Tim. 2:1-3)."

We may not agree with our leaders. We may be forced to live in oppression and reap the consequences of evil leadership, but we can be assured that God is the One who sees and will repay in His time.

We, as God's people, are instructed to pray for those in power because He can still move the heart of any man. Just imagine what would happen if we all prayed instead of complaining. God would without doubt hear and answer those prayers, and we might see a positive change in the way our communities are governed. Just a thought and note to self.

WHAT PRAYERS ARE YOU PRAYING FOR YOUR LEADERS TODAY?

DAY 59

PSALM 59:16

"But I will sing of your strength, in the morning I will sing of your love; for you are my fortress, my refuge in times of trouble."

~*~

[David's prayer for deliverance from the men Saul had sent to kill him. The psalmist also expresses his confidence in God who hears and will answer his cries for help.]

Once again, David is petitioning the Lord to save him from his enemy, King Saul. And, in this verse, he is reminding God that even though he wants his enemies defeated...even though his heart is anxious because of their constant plans against him, David has resolved in his heart to again focus his attention on the One who protects and provides. For David, God is his song and his inner joy. The Lord gives David strength when he is at his breaking point.

David will begin each day with a song sung in praise and adoration for his God because God is his fortress. He knows he can run to the Lord in prayer, and God knows every anxious thought even before

David utters a word.

Even in human terms, a physical fortress is immovable; it cannot be shaken. But our God is even more immovable, and on every level whether it be physical, mental, spiritual or emotional. He cannot be moved or thrown off course by man's evil deeds or by situations which seem impossible.

We, like David, can run to God to find safety and solace no matter what the problem. We can sing His praise.

Are you needing a place of safety and rest? Run to Him! He will put a new song in your heart and be your point of comfort.

HOW HAS GOD BEEN YOUR FORTRESS AND REFUGE? WHY NOT WRITE OUT A SONG OF PRAISE TO HIM TODAY?

DAY 60

"You have rejected us, O God, and burst forth upon us; you have been angry—now restore us!"

~*~

[A song put to the music of "The Lily of the Covenant," praying for God's help and victory in a time of war with Edom.]

David is acknowledging that Israel has sinned, and God has allowed their enemies to gain the upper hand.

The mere fact that David recognizes they have been cast off, however, is key. His heart is tender enough to understand that he and his people are not where they should be.

There is a more tragic situation, though—those who do not realize they've been set aside at all. When people reject God and His ways for too long, eventually they will be cast off, their hearts hardened, and they will be abandoned and left to their own devices.

We do not completely understand God's inner-workings, but we know that as long as we still sense right from wrong; still see our sin for what it is and repent of it, then we can come to the Father and receive forgiveness and restoration.

Today, if you sense you have drifted from God, then fight your way back to Him. Just as David acknowledged his sin and the sins of his people, only with God as our banner, can we find true victory.

HAVE YOU EVER FELT REJECTED BY GOD? WHAT DO YOU THINK WAS THE REASON BEHIND IT?

DAY 61

"Hear my cry, O God; listen to my prayer. From the ends of the earth I call to you, I call as my heart grows faint; lead me to the rock that is higher than I. For you have been my refuge, a strong tower against the foe. I long to dwell in your tent forever and take refuge in the shelter of your wings."

~*~

[This song is a prayer of restoration to God's presence. It was quite possibly written when David had been driven out or banished by Saul or Absalom.]

David had been driven out of his kingdom and is calling unto God to protect and restore. He understands that there is no place too desolate or far away for God to hear his cry.

Likewise, God is our rock, that mighty fortress we cling to in times of trouble; and He provides protection from our enemies. Like a child crying out for the safety of his daddy's arms, David knows that where God dwells no evil can befall him. He longs to live in that perfect place which offers eternal security, and he likens it to the warmth and protection of a chick nestled underneath the mother hen's wing.

When you and I feel as if we have been pushed into the outer limits, God is our shelter. He is our rock of protection and deliverance. When we become overwhelmed by life, may we run to Him and feel His perfect love and strengthening, just like David did. The psalmist's words should become our battle cry, "Lead me to the rock that is higher than I."

WHO IS THE FIRST ONE YOU RUN TO WHEN A PROBLEM ARISES?

DAY 62

"Find rest, O my soul, in God alone; my hope comes from him."

~*~

[This song is David's commitment to rest in God despite the threats continuously bombarding him.]

Few people like to wait. I am probably the most impatient person, but I have learned that God never gets in a hurry with anything.

David was encouraging himself to wait on God to move and act on his behalf. He knew in his heart that God was trustworthy and would not fail to bring about His plans for the shepherd king. So, David waited expectantly and remembered that God had David's best interests at heart.

When you and I get in a hurry and rush forward with what we think is best, we often find ourselves miserable or lacking in our desires. But we must remember that God can bring about the right opportunity, the right person, or the right path at the exact and perfect time, therefore, we must wait on God to act.

What or who are you waiting on today? Be still. Allow God time to work out everything for His greater purpose. You will see, if you rest patiently, He will work out the details in ways you would not or could not have imagined.

WHAT ARE YOU WAITING ON TODAY AND WHAT IS GOD SPEAKING TO YOU IN THE WAIT?

DAY 63

PSALM 63:1

"O God, you are my God, earnestly I seek you; my soul thirsts for you, my body longs for you, in a dry and weary land where there is no water."

~*~

[This song of David expresses a deep longing for God, especially when enemies threaten. God's presence brings security, and with that, David could experience peace and, ultimately, joy.]

David was in the wilderness of Judah possibly running from his son, Absalom. He was not only far from the comforts of his court, but away from those reminders of God's goodness and His presence.

In some translations it mentions David seeking God early; in other words, David not only met with God in prayer each morning, but that meeting was the first thing of his day and done with eagerness. David's body and soul were weary, and nothing in this world could truly satisfy the longing he felt gnawing at his bones.

I think we all can relate. This world leaves us empty. We might find temporary pleasure or satisfaction, but then the feeling of longing returns. We are left spiritually thirsty with nothing to satisfy.

David understood that the only One who could truly quench his thirst was God. Likewise, we, too, must come to the realization we are never going to find complete satisfaction here from this world. We are just passing through, and we have one shot...one life in which to grab hold of the living water.

Jesus was and is that living water. He declared to the woman at the well, "...but whoever drinks the water I give him will never thirst. Indeed, the water I give him will become in him a spring of water welling up to eternal life" (John 4:14)..

So, let me ask, have you tasted of the living water? If not, reach out for Him today. He's waiting to fill you. **DO YOU HAVE A DEEP INNER THIRST? IS THIS WORLD LEAVING YOU DRY? WHY NOT CALL OUT TO HIM?**

DAY 64

PSALM 64:7A

"But God..."

~*~

[David is pleading with God regarding his enemies who had caused him much trouble. His reflection is summed up in the two words, "But God." Without Him, David would not have withstood the continuous attacks.]

It is never good practice to settle on just a few words in scripture without understanding the entire context behind them. In this instance, however, David's words, "but God," display a shift in his petition.

David was pleading with God to protect him from those who would conspire against him and form malicious words which cut right to the heart. In verse 7, the writer transforms his focus by describing the action God would take, and the psalmist starts it off with these simple words...*but God.*

Sometimes you and I need to refocus and insert a "but God" into our situation. Yes, we may be experiencing heartache and hard times...but God. Yes, this season in our life is difficult...but God. True the outcome looks bleak...but God. Where is your faith, friend? He's not finished yet. He's only getting started!

Though the mountains be shaken, and the hills be removed, God reminds us that His unfailing love will *not* falter, for He is a God of great compassion! (Is. 54:10)

When our life is upside down, the time is ripe for God to step in and do His most incredible work. If you are His child, then He delights in you and will use even the most challenging moments for His glory and your greater good.

So, chin up. Look for your "but God" today. He is sufficient.

HOW DO YOU NEED GOD TO STEP IN TODAY? JUST WAIT. HE WILL.

DAY 65

PSALM 65:5

"You answer us with awesome deeds of righteousness, O God our Savior, the hope of all the ends of the earth and of the farthest seas,"

~*~

[This song is a hymn of praise to God for all He has done for His people, both by forgiving their sins and by directing the affairs of the world so they may have peace.]

Do you journal? I like to journal from time to time to write down and remember the things God has done for my family and for me. My journal is almost like a history book of situations and circumstances where, in my eyes, there was no hope, but in God's hands, He somehow made a way.

In this psalm, David is giving glory to God for His gracious acts towards man within His temple and upon the earth. He writes...

You hear prayer...

You forgave our transgressions...

You choose and bring near...

You fill...

You answer…
You formed…
You stilled the roaring seas…
You call…
You care for the land…
You enrich it…
You water it…
You soften it…
You give bounty…

These are all action phrases that describe God at work as He cares for His creation. Who can compare? Sometimes I think we forget God is constantly working on our behalf, and until we can sit still and reflect like David did of all the things He has done or is doing, we underestimate God's love for us.

Today, make time to create a list. Note all the good things, the people, God's blessings He has given to you. These are all out of the love He has for you. I think you'll be surprised how much He has provided, but also how much we take for granted.

DO YOU KEEP A JOURNAL? WHAT TYPES OF THINGS DO YOU WRITE ABOUT?

Day 66

Psalm 66:16

"Come and listen, all you who fear God; let me tell you what he has done for me."

~*~

[This is a song of Thanksgiving. All of God's people are called to sing His praises.]

Each year on Christmas Eve, thousands of people gather in churches to sing about and celebrate the birth of God's Son. It is a special occasion. All come dressed in their Christmas finery, families come together for the special evening event, and there is a hint of excitement in the air. What if this was not just a yearly thing? What if each of us experienced worship this way each time we gathered?

Per the psalmist's words, the heart cry of every believer across the world should be, Come! Listen! Ring the bell! Let me tell you what God has done! He was calling on people to praise God for all His works both out of duty and delight, and to give glory for the things already accomplished and those yet to come!

At Christmas we celebrate and honor the greatest gift ever given, so let us give praise and thanks *every* day for this most precious and costly gift. For through Jesus' sacrifice on the cross, He paved the way for us to have a restored and personal relationship with Almighty God!

Come! Listen! Let me tell you all about Him!!

ARE YOU TELLING OTHERS ABOUT WHAT GOD HAS DONE IN YOUR LIFE?

DAY 67

"May God be gracious to us and bless us and make his face shine upon us, that your ways may be known on earth, your salvation among all nations."

~*~

[This song is a prayer that the salvation and praises of the Lord will spread throughout all the earth.]

I don't know if you have ever attended a missionary commissioning ceremony, but there is something special about those who have surrendered to God's calling to leave their life behind and go where He is sending them. This psalm was a type of commissioning and David was speaking on behalf of the people. It was his desire for the good news of God's salvation to be spread to all nations.

Some translations begin verse 1 by saying, "May God be merciful to us." Mercy is where blessing begins. Forgiveness of our sins is the first stop to the Lord's favor.

The church cries out for God's mercy to not just abound in us, but in the whole world! May they *all* hear what the Lord has done for them! All have been offered salvation and can come and receive His great blessing.

My prayer today is that you and I will recognize God's graciousness. He has offered the gift of mercy if we will only accept it. May we, just as in the words of David's prayer, do our part to tell others and celebrate what the Lord has done!

PRAY FOR, OFFER SUPPORT, AND ENCOURAGE MISSIONARIES EVERY DAY.

DAY 68

PSALM 68:5-6

"A father to the fatherless, a defender of widows, is God in his holy dwelling. God sets the lonely in families, he leads out the prisoners with singing; but the rebellious live in a sun-scorched land."

~*~

[This psalm written by David, was probably sung when he brought the ark from the house of Obed-edom to the place in Zion he had set up for the Lord.]

I love this passage as it displays the tenderness of God. Here, David tributes God as a "father to the fatherless" and a "defender of widows." When people express their faith in God, the Lord remains present when others step away or are permanently removed. He provides and meets every need of these vulnerable ones. He blesses them, provides, comforts, teaches, and defends them, and they can count on Him to never leave them empty handed.

God also sets the lonely in families. He champions for those who have none in their lives to offer companionship and encouragement, and places them among people who will welcome them.

Finally, God sets free those who have been imprisoned either by someone else's hand or their own, such as He did with the Israelites who were in bondage to the Egyptians. Yet, He leaves the rebellious—those who willfully have turned away from Him—desperately wanting in an empty, dry land (life).

So, as David would later write..." The LORD is gracious and compassionate, slow to anger and rich in love (Ps. 145:8)." Indeed.

IN THIS PASSAGE OF PSALM 68:5-6, WHICH SECTION SPEAKS THE LOUDEST TO YOU AT THIS POINT IN YOUR LIFE? CONTEMPLATE WHY AND REFLECT ON THE SITUATION THAT IS EITHER NOW RESOLVED (AND THANK GOD FOR THAT RESOLUTION) OR STILL NEEDS TO BE CONFRONTED (AND PRAY FOR THE WISDOM AND MEANS TO RESOLVE THE SITUATION).

DAY 69

PSALM 69:1-3

"Save me, O God, for the waters have come up to my neck. I sink in the miry depths, where there is no foothold. I have come into the deep waters; the floods engulf me. I am worn out calling for help; my throat is parched. My eyes fail, looking for my God."

~*~

[Chapter 69 is David crying out in his affliction, but also in some of the verses, a reflection of Christ-like sufferings.]

Probably, at some point, we all have felt as if we are drowning in troubles. David was no exception.

In the above passage, we see a few main points:

David knows where his help comes from.

His circumstances are bigger than David but not larger than God.

He is weak and weary, but he does not falter in his faith.

David's reactions in this passage, were so contrary to how the world responds. Every day I see people going through huge life battles, yet many have no hope, no one to turn to, and no source of relief. Why?

Because they walk alone. They have ignored or refused the love and help of their Creator.

But, I've also had a front-row seat to those who are suffering endless trials, yet their season of trial has a different air to it. They suffer, yes, but with hope. They understand the hardship is temporary. Their eyes are fixed upward, and their trust is completely in God's greater plan within their pain.

David embraced his afflictions. Though the difficulties were not welcomed, he understood they served a purpose and therefore God would see him through to the other side of the suffering.

Whatever you are walking through today, know that there is One who wants to carry your burdens if you will let Him.

If He is already a dear Friend, then press on. He will give you the strength you need in your momentary trials.

DO YOU HAVE THE HOPE THAT GOD GIVES? IS THERE SOMEONE YOU KNOW WHO NEEDS TO HEAR ABOUT THAT HOPE TODAY?

DAY 70

PSALM 70:5

"Yet I am poor and needy; come quickly to me, O God. You are my help and my deliverer; O LORD, do not delay."

~*~

[David's urgent prayer for help when threatened by his enemies.]

It is human nature to seek immediate relief from our trials and pain. Hurry, God! Fix this! Do not delay! That was David's cry; yet as we have discovered in many other verses, though God did sometimes come to David's aid quickly, it did not always happen quickly. Does this mean He doesn't care? No. It means there are lessons to be learned within the trials.

If a young sapling never experiences the pressures of the wind against its trunk and branches, the roots will never anchor deeply into the soil, and shallow roots make a tree more vulnerable to toppling as it grows larger.

Our trials help to mold and shape our character. David experienced many trials in his lifetime, but each one made him into the great king he became—a man after God's own heart.

David learned to trust God; to rely on Him for protection and provision. He learned that his own strength and prowess could take him only so far, but God's strength and supply knows no bounds.

Truly, man cannot save himself. You and I must rely on God to work all things out for our good. And so, we, like David, say, "O LORD, do not delay!"

HAS THERE BEEN A TIME IN YOUR LIFE WHEN YOU FELT AS IF GOD WAS NOT MOVING QUICK ENOUGH? WHAT DID YOU DO?

DAY 71

"Even when I am old and gray, do not forsake me, O God, till I declare your power to the next generation, your might to all who are to come."

~*~

[A prayer of the psalmist—quite possibly David—to sustain and help him in his older years.]

I have a friend, now in her eighties, who despite physical ailments and family disappointments, lives Jesus out loud for all to see. I've admired her tenacity and grit, but most importantly her love for her Savior.

Perhaps you, too, have known an older person who has faithfully served God all their years, and even now, body bent and mind not as sharp, still calls out to God for His faithful love and support.

These penned words of Psalm 71:18, are a beautiful reminder of how we never outgrow God. The psalmist prayed even, in the latter years of his life when his physical strength was waning, that the Lord would not "azab" (Hebrew for "leave") him but would give opportunity for the psalmist to declare God's power to the next generation, thereby supplying a legacy of faith. Wow! How many older folks do you and I know who still have the zeal of this psalmist?

He understood that his years were ending but wanted desperately to tell those coming up behind him about God Who had never failed him. If only we had this kind of faith!

Today, in whatever season of life you are in, God is not finished with you yet. Until your final breath, it is your duty and privilege to tell the next generation about the goodness and mercy of the Lord. So, there are your marching orders, foot soldier, start marching!

HAVE YOU KNOWN AN OLDER PERSON WHO STILL LIVES OUT THEIR FAITH IN AMAZING WAYS? HOW DID THEIR EXAMPLE AFFECT YOU?

DAY 72

PSALM 72:6

"He will be like rain falling on a mown field, like showers watering the earth."

~*~

[This chapter includes the last words of David believed to have been penned by his son, Solomon.]

Christ and His future reign on the earth is the subject here. The earth has gone spiritually thirsty long enough, and now the psalmist looks forward to God's glorious healing waters which will soothe the dry ground and burdened hearts like the Great Balm of Gilead. Gilead was known for its herbal remedies, and as with many of the psalms, this verse also foretells of Jesus coming to heal the world's wounds.

You and I need this healing balm! We walk through so much heartache, and it leaves us feeling dry, parched, and in dire need of God's refreshment. When we turn to Him, He lovingly showers us with His goodness, grace, sustaining mercy, and strength. Without Him we would wither, as so many unfortunately do.

I am not sure what you are walking through

today. Many people have experienced hard things over the past couple of years. Why not turn to the healing Balm and refresh in His holy goodness?

Remember the call of Jesus..." Come to Me, all you who are weary and burdened, and I will give you rest (Matt. 11:28)."

IF YOU ARE NEEDING SOME REFRESHMENT FOR YOUR SOUL TODAY TAKE A FEW MOMENTS TO CONSIDER HOW RAIN NOURISHES WILD FLOWERS AND FORESTS WITHOUT THE NEED FOR MAN'S INTERVENTION. JUST AS GOD PROVIDES FOR THIS IN NATURE, HE WILL ALSO REFRESH YOU IF YOU'RE OPEN TO HIS NOURISHMENT.

DAY 73

"When I tried to understand all this, it was oppressive to me till I entered the sanctuary of God; then I understood their final destiny."

~*~

[The psalmist here, is Asaph, the chief musician during David's reign.]

Asaph was frustrated by the fact that the wicked seemed to prosper without consequence, while he experienced hardship and turmoil. His complaint: is living a godly life worth it?

Can you relate? I know I have had these same thoughts at times. But then…

Asaph went into the house of God. His envy was dismissed as he realized the depraved condition of those whom he had once looked upon with contempt and jealousy. A time was coming when God would righteously judge their waywardness, and they would be swiftly escorted to their eternal ruin.

Asaph ends his psalm with these words, "Those who are far from you will perish; you destroy all who are unfaithful to you. But as for me, it is good to be near God. I have made the Sovereign Lord my refuge; I will tell of all your deeds (vs.27-28)."

Through reflection and understanding, Asaph's attitude had been adjusted and his focus rearranged. We, too, often need to shift our gazes back on God and the eternal instead of what temporal gain others may seem to have. If we have security in the Lord, then we have all we need.

HAVE YOU EVER QUESTIONED GOD WHEN UNBELIEVERS SEEM TO HAVE IT ALL AND YOU ARE LEFT STRUGGLING? HOW DO YOU HANDLE THOSE FEELINGS?

DAY 74

"How long will the enemy mock you, O God? Will the foe revile your name forever?"

~*~

[This psalm was written as a lament and complaint to God regarding the destruction of Jerusalem and the temple by Nebuchadnezzar and the army of the Chaldeans.]

The words of Asaph, here, reflect the heart of believers everywhere, even unto today…

How long, God?

Just as Asaph questioned in Psalm 73, it sometimes seems as though those who are opposed to God and to good in general have the upper hand. Almost as if the Lord has no power or will to retaliate or save His glory and honor.

Yet, this is exactly a quality of God we will never completely understand. The Bible tells us in Psalm 103:8, "The LORD is compassionate and gracious, slow to anger, abounding in love." Additionally, "The Lord is not slow in keeping his promise, as some understand slowness. Instead, he is patient with you, not wanting anyone to perish, but everyone to come to repentance (2 Peter 3:9)."

Do not be mistaken, the Lord is omnipotent and there will be just judgment upon those who have continually hardened their hearts and ignored His invitation for salvation. In the meantime, His grace and mercy are immeasurable. He is long-suffering and He gives ample opportunity for you and me to reject our sinful, stubborn ways and turn to Him.

I don't know about you, but there is only One who deserves all honor and praise!

HOW CAN YOU WAIT PATIENTLY FOR THE LORD TO REDEEM HIS NAME?

DAY 75

PSALM 75:7

"But it is God who judges: He brings one down, he exalts another."

~*~

[Words from Asaph that reflect some of David's similar thoughts. Asaph opens the chapter with praise, and then proceeds to display God's righteousness in positioning or deposing leaders. The psalmist ends with his dedication to the Lord.]

Leaders and kingdoms come and go, and as the writer of this psalm portrays, it is not by the people's own hand, but by the Will of God. People have no actual control but that which the Lord has allowed.

Larry W. Wilson from Wake-Up Seminars says, "Civilizations come and go, and governments rise and fall. Because our Creator loves people, He also blesses each nation with a span of time so it might prosper and do well, but this blessing ends when a nation becomes degenerate, rebellious, and unfit for self-rule. When God determines that extended mercy for a nation has no redeeming effect, He marginalizes or destroys that nation." [3]

This psalm is a good reminder to us not to get too comfortable with our position in life. Though we have been blessed tremendously, those advantages can all be taken away just as quickly as they were given. This psalm also challenges us to pray for our leaders. It is crucial that our leaders maintain integrity and have lives which seek God and His will. Our prayers can help change the hearts of men and women in power.

HOW HAVE YOU SEEN GOD WORK AND MOVE THROUGH MEMBERS OF OUR GOVERNMENT OR OTHER TYPES OF LEADERSHIP?

---

[3] "God Raises Up Kings or Nations and Removes Them," Larry W. Wilson, https://wake-up.org/morality/god-raises-up-kings-or-nations-and-removes-them-larry-w-wilson.html.

DAY 76

"Valiant men lie plundered, they sleep their last sleep; not one of the warriors can lift his hands. At your rebuke, O God of Jacob, both horse and chariot lie still. You alone are to be feared. Who can stand before you when you are angry?"

~*~

[This is a celebratory psalm of God's invincible power against those who would come against Jerusalem.]

There are numerous accounts of strange happenings on the battlefield when those who come against God's people have been repelled. Consider the protecting pillar of cloud between Pharoah's army and the fleeing Israelites in the book of Exodus. God does fight on His people's behalf.

The Bible tells us God protects His own. This does not mean bad things never happen, but it does mean there comes a point when He says, "enough!"

Here a mighty army has come to war against His people, but these warriors have no power when the Lord is in the fight. God has all but silenced them and they are no more.

We fight spiritual battles every day, and we must remember these things when we are in those tense moments. Call upon the name of the Lord, for He is our Mighty Warrior able to save. He has the power to silence any foe and bring peace where once there was chaos; deliverance in our time of trouble. GREAT is His Name!

HOW HAS THE LORD FOUGHT FOR YOU THIS WEEK?

DAY 77

PSALM 77:1-2

*"I cried out to God for help; I cried out to God to hear me.
When I was in distress, I sought the Lord; at night I
stretched out untiring hands, and my soul refused to be
comforted."*

~*~

**[A song of Asaph including both sorrowful
complaints and uplifting encouragement.]**

The psalmist is deeply troubled. He raises his
complaints to God, but even in the watches of the
night, he is restless and refuses to be comforted.

Sometimes we are like this psalmist. We become
overburdened with the troubles of this life, and though
we may air our complaints to God, we do not fully
release them into His care. Often when we cannot see
Him working, or we do not receive answers right away
and we grow frustrated and begin questioning if God
even realizes our distress.

The psalmist, after reflection on past miraculous
workings of the Lord, finally concludes that God's
ways are holy. He pauses to remember how the Lord
has displayed His power in the lives of the Psalmist's

ancestors and so he affirms that God can and will do it again. He rejoices in remembering the good, instead of allowing the current troubling situation to overcome his spirit.

If you are struggling with fears, anxiety, frustrations, etc., take a moment to reflect on the times God has worked in miraculous ways on your behalf, and then tell yourself with confidence that He will do it again.

ARE YOU DEEPLY TROUBLED BY SOMETHING TODAY? GIVE IT TO GOD AND TRUST HE WILL COME THROUGH.

DAY 78

PSALM 78:3-4

"…what we have heard and known, what our fathers have told us. We will not hide them from their children; we will tell the next generation the praiseworthy deeds of the Lord, his power, and the wonders he has done."

~*~

[This Psalm of Asaph describes the merciful acts of God towards a rebellious people.]

Time and again, God steps in and miraculously works on behalf of His people, Israel; but so often, they stubbornly turn away and forget Who gave them all they had.

In verses three and four, Asaph declares that the people have an awesome responsibility to tell the next generation about God and all His deeds. They need not only to tell others, but to remind themselves about the goodness of God.

These verses should offer a challenge to us today. We are commanded to teach our children about God. If we do not, we will be no different than the Israelites who fell away and, except for a remnant, were eventually destroyed because of their lack of knowledge and faith.

As the Psalmist later states: "they did not keep God's covenant and refused to live by his law. They forgot what he had done, the wonders he had shown them (vs. 10-11)." "So he ended their days in futility and their years in terror (vs. 33)."

May we never forget or neglect to teach our children about the Lord and all He has done for us. May we be a people of faith who boldly declares His truths to all.

HOW CAN YOU MAKE SURE THE NEXT GENERATION KNOWS ABOUT GOD?

DAY 79

"…may your mercy come quickly to meet us, for we are in desperate need."

~*~

[Asaph alerts the distress signal. Jerusalem is under siege (or has been destroyed) and now he pleads with God to return the favor to those who have trampled on the city and temple.]

Sometimes we find ourselves in a situation where we are desperate for any kind of help. Without God's intervention, we sit in nothing but ruins, and we cry out to God, "Come quickly, Lord!"

Perhaps our trials come at the hands of others or are there by our own doing, but unless something happens or someone steps in, we see no hope. Yet, God is faithful. He knows how long the trial should run its course to get us in a place of humble submission. He knows our absolute breaking point. He understands what it is that will mold and shape our will to bend to His.

Friend, He hears you. He sees us. If we turn to Him and cry out, He will answer. Asaph knew God would step in, and he declared, "Then we your people, the sheep of your pasture, will praise you forever; from generation to generation we will recount your praise (vs. 13)."

Has God stepped in for you? Has He altered your situation for the better? Then praise Him. If you are still waiting, praise Him for what He will do for you in the future. He will do the unbelievable on your behalf. Just wait!

WHAT ARE YOU WAITING ON TODAY? PRAISE HIM FOR THE ANSWER TO COME!

DAY 80

"Restore us, O God; make your face shine upon us, that we may be saved."

~*~

[Chapter 80 is a prayer for Israel's restoration after having been destroyed by a foreign power. And why? Because they had turned away from God.]

Have you ever felt as if God were angry or disappointed with you? Perhaps you did something you knew was wrong, or maybe you did not do what He was calling you to do. Unpleasant are the moments you realize we've not heeded God's call, but it is at those moments that you and I must cry out to Him in repentance. He is always ready to forgive and is able to take us back and lift our head.

We have all fallen away at some point. This psalmist's cry is one every believer should be quick to utter. Turn to us again!

Turn us back to You, God. Make our focus be on You and not ourselves. Turn us back, God, to that electric faith which gave us a drive and passion to see the lost saved. Turn us back, Father, to have a heart for

Your people; to care about those who are hurting and downtrodden.

Spurgeon says this: "The best turn is not that of circumstances but of character. When the Lord turns His people, He will soon turn their condition. It needs the Lord Himself to do this, for conversion is as divine a work as creation; and those who have been once turned unto God, if they at any time backslide, as much need the Lord to turn them again as to turn them at the first."[4]

Just imagine how differently this nation, our churches, and our homes would look if we all turned back to God.

HOW DO YOU NEED GOD TO RESTORE YOU TODAY? IS YOUR FAITH SHAKY? HAVE YOU LOST YOUR PASSION FOR HIM? ASK HIM TO STEP IN AND CHANGE THINGS. HE WILL.

---

[4] "Knowing God Through His Word Day by Day," Pam Larson, https://bible-daily.org/2021/04/10/restore-us-o-god/.

DAY 81

PSALM 81:11-14

"'But my people would not listen to me; Israel would not submit to me. So I gave them over to their stubborn hearts to follow their own devices. If my people would only listen to me, if Israel would only follow my ways, how quickly I would subdue their enemies and turn my hand against their foes!'"

~*~

[This psalm is a recollection of how God's chosen people—those He had brought out of bondage, hardened their hearts to a point that He had no alternative but to step aside and allow them to suffer the consequences of their free will...and their sin.]

Many have found themselves in this very spot. Because God gives us free will and the ability to choose, He allows us to make our own decisions even if it means we create more problems and more heartache for ourselves and others.

If we take a closer look, those who put their faith and trust in God and continually seek Him throughout their lifetime, find that God is near and always hears their prayers for help or assistance. However, those who harden their hearts and continuously step outside the will of God, have placed themselves in a precarious and dangerous position. God's protection is no longer with them, and, in fact, because He is not welcome in their lives, He hands them over to their own depraved state.

Today, may we not harden our hearts, but rather submit to His Lordship and leadership. God sees the whole picture where we see only a minuscule portion. When we allow Him to lead, He will take us places we never fathomed; He will give us wisdom and discernment to make the best choices in life.

ARE YOU LISTENING WELL TO GOD? IF NOT, ASK HIM TO HELP YOU GET TO A PLACE OF TOTAL SURRENDER.

DAY 82

PSALM 82:5

"They know nothing, they understand nothing. They walk about in darkness; all the foundations of the earth are shaken."

~*~

[This Psalm of Asaph is referring to magistrates or judges who were ruling unjustly. They had forgotten that their word was not the ultimate authority, but rather God has final say. These judges were neither defending the cause of the weak nor maintaining the rights of the oppressed. Asaph was warning them that a higher judgment would come from the God Who presides over His heavenly court.]

This same scenario is played out daily within our own society. We the people have, at times, foolishly elected power-hungry men and women who care not for those over whom they preside, but look only to their own agendas and interests.

Spurgeon says that it is, "A wretched plight for a nation to be in when its justices know no justice, and its judges are devoid of judgment."[5]

When the justices are more crooked than the people whom they serve, a nation is on shaky ground. Thus, the reason we must wisely choose, through prayer and petition, who presides in the hallowed halls of our government.

Today, let us pray for those who are in a seat of authority. Let us petition God to bring back integrity and a sense of awe for the position. May those who judge do so with a deep desire to fulfill God's commands in every situation.

PRAY FOR THOSE WHO HAVE LOST THEIR RIGHTS UNJUSTLY, AND FOR THOSE WHO ARE APPOINTED TO SIT IN JUDGMENT TODAY, AND EVERY DAY.

---

[5] "Equity or Equality," Darrell B. Harrison, https://justthinking.me/equity-or-equality/.

DAY 83

"'Come,' they say, 'let us destroy them as a nation, that the name of Israel be remembered no more.'"

~*~

[Asaph's Psalm is a prayer for God to wipe out the enemies of His beloved Israel who had seemingly all come against her.]

It is nothing new. The people of God have always been a target for those who want to silence them, and Israel has been a nation of contempt since the very early days of its setting apart and miraculous retrieval from the hands of the Egyptians. The Bible refers to the people of God as "the apple of His eye (Zechariah 2:8)," and He will never cease to hold a remnant from His people.

Further, Psalm 83:4 also reflects that man will try to silence those who have the truth and who call others out according to their sin. Evil cannot tolerate good. Spurgeon writes, "Men would be glad to cast the church out of the world because it rebukes them and is thus a standing menace to their sinful peace."

Oh, but may we continue to stand strong and be a

beacon of hope and light to an ever-darkening world. God's people may be battered, but they will not be defeated. Ultimately, Christ will sound the battle cry and He will reign victorious! Soli Deo Gloria! (To God alone be the glory!)

DO YOU MAKE IT A PRACTICE TO PRAY FOR ALL THE COUNTRIES OF THE WORLD TO TURN TO GOD?

DAY 84

"For the Lord God is a sun and shield; the Lord bestows favor and honor. No good thing does he withhold from those whose walk is blameless."

~*~

[Psalm 84 is a song of peace and longing for God's temple.]

Throughout history, there have been many who waffled between a relationship with God and a falling away. Take for example the ancient Israelite people. They would draw close to God, and He would listen, provide provisions, protection, and favor. However, there were times when they fell away from their faith and into idol worship or no worship at all. It was during those moments of unfaithfulness when God allowed them to be overtaken by others until they recognized their disobedience and turned back to Him. This psalm clearly demonstrates that God's favor rests on those who seek Him.

God is both sun and shield for those who love Him. The former is in times of peace when He enlightens and guides the people. The latter in times of trouble when He becomes that shield and shelter from the fiery darts of the evil one.

God delights in blessing and lifting up those who seek Him, by giving grace and glory, and He withholds no blessings which are for our greater good or His higher purpose. Our job is to stay close and not stray; to keep Him the center of our daily lives.

With Him as our Lord, we will not falter, for He is the LORD Almighty and as the psalmist declares in verse twelve, "blessed is the one who trusts in You!" May we once again put God first and see His favor on display.

HOW HAS GOD DISPLAYED HIS FAVOR ON YOU AND YOUR FAMILY?

DAY 85

PSALM 85:6

"Will you not revive us again, that your people may rejoice in you?"

~*~

[Psalm 85 is a prayer from an afflicted nation for God's former mercies, with the belief and hope that they will see it again.]

Years ago, tent revivals were all the rage. Tents would be set up and for days and people would gather to hear the Word of God preached. The intense preaching, praise, and worship led to people learning about salvation and giving their hearts to God. Revival of the heart is a total dependence on God.

The heart cry for revival has rolled off many lips throughout history, and God has accomplished this magnificent feat because He is still the same God now that He was in years past. It is not an impossible request. His grace has converted whole communities (think of Jonah and Ninevah).

The cry for revival takes the focus off us and places it all on Him—the Giver. It follows with shouts of praise for all He is about to do. God loves when His children turn back to Him and are filled with a joy overflowing.

May we be like the psalmist of this song and implore God to revive us, our church, and our communities again. Oh, that we may once again be filled with His wellspring of joy and healing!

HAVE YOU FELT THE NEED FOR REVIVAL IN YOUR OWN LIFE AND CONSCIENTIOUSLY LOOKED FOR A RENEWAL OF SPIRIT FROM GOD? IF NOT, WHAT'S STOPPING YOU?

DAY 86

PSALM 86:11

"Teach me Your way, O LORD, and I will walk in Your truth; give me an undivided heart, that I may fear your name."

~*~

[A prayer of David.]

David was a king with a lot of life experiences and wisdom, yet he understood that he still needed to learn more from the One whose knowledge is limitless.

In our own lives, questions loom: which way should we go? Which job should we take? Where should we live? What church is best for our families? Like David, we should seek God for His truth. He has the answers, but it is our job to search for them. This means spending time in prayer every day; to study the Bible regularly; and not to forego meeting together with other believers. God uses each of these activities to show us the right way and provide answers to our questions.

"Give me an undivided heart."

Having a heart that is solely fixed and fixated on Him is what God desires for us. We cannot have one foot in heavenly places and the other in the world. We must be all-in, in one or the other, for when our hearts are divided, we will not make right choices, nor will we be able to clearly discern God's will for our lives.

As with David, we must ask God to give us an undivided heart so that we can be fixated solely on Him.

WOULD YOU SAY THAT YOU HAVE AN UNDIVIDED HEART? IF NOT, WHAT STEPS CAN YOU TAKE TO GET RE-FOCUSED?

DAY 87

"The LORD will write in the register of the peoples: 'This one was born in Zion.' Selah."

~*~

[This is a song with both a religious and patriotic tone referring to Zion—Jerusalem—the city of God's people. It was either composed or dedicated to the sons of Korah, who kept the doors of the house of the Lord.]

This verse, though seemingly minuscule, has great meaning. It refers to the event in time when the Lord will sort out the people one from another; those who belong to Him and those who do not believe in Him.

In the book of Matthew, Chapter 25:31-46, Jesus tells of a time when He will sit on His glorious throne and will sort the sheep from the goats, referring to people. Those who belong to and follow Him will be placed on His right side. Those who reject Him and His ways will be positioned on the left.

The people on the right will then receive their eternal reward in heaven with Him. Those on the left will be thrown into eternal punishment in hell. That is difficult to hear, but it is a truth we all need to grasp.

Jesus, while delivering His famous Sermon on the Mount, said these words, "Not everyone who says to me, 'Lord, Lord,' will enter the kingdom of heaven, but only the one who does the will of my Father who is in heaven. Many will say to me on that day, 'Lord, Lord, did we not prophesy in your name and in your name drive out demons and perform many miracles?' Then I will tell them plainly, 'I never knew you. Away from me, you evildoers!' (Matthew 7:21-23)"

WHICH SIDE ARE YOU ON TODAY? HAVE YOU MADE THAT DECISION TO FOLLOW JESUS? DO YOU NEED HELP OR HAVE QUESTIONS? REACH OUT TO SOMEONE TODAY AND EITHER DISCOVER OR SHARE THE GOOD NEWS OF THE GOSPEL MESSAGE!

DAY 88

"O LORD, the God who saves me; day and night I cry out before you. May my prayer come before you; turn your ear to my cry. For my soul is full of trouble and my life draws near the grave."

~*~

[Psalm 88 is a lamentation of the writer's own personal troubles. It is the most woeful of all the psalms.]

As we have travelled through the Psalms, perhaps you have noticed the large amount of desperation, sadness, and complaint from the pen of the psalmists. These words could be viewed as depressing if it were not for the hope sprinkled in amongst the cries for help.

Psalm 88 is no different, yet you and I know there is so much relatable truth here. This life can dish out a lot of sad things, and we, like the psalm writers, often find ourselves overwhelmed, heartbroken, and desperate for relief. Our world is broken, and there is only One who can fix it. There is only One who can right the wrongs, bind up the wounds, and bring beauty from ashes.

The psalmist, though heavy with despair, realized his hope and salvation came from the Lord. And, like this psalmist, so many people today are the walking wounded, trying to find anything which might relieve them of their burdens. They come up short, and often there is nothing left to live for. Please hear me: God is the answer. Nothing will satisfy like the Savior. No one can heal like Jesus, who sticks closer than a brother.

So today, I urge you to seek Him. He's waiting with open arms to carry that burden for you. He's big enough. He's ready and waiting.

ARE YOU WEIGHED DOWN BY HEARTACHES THE WORLD HAS DISHED OUT? WHAT STEPS WILL YOU TAKE TODAY TO GET YOU BACK ON TRACK?

DAY 89

PSALM 89:33-37

"...but I will not take my love from him, nor will I ever betray my faithfulness. I will not violate my covenant or alter what my lips have uttered. Once for all, I have sworn by my holiness— and I will not lie to David— that his line will continue forever and his throne endure before me like the sun; it will be established forever like the moon, the faithful witness in the sky."

~*~

[Psalm 89 is a prayer of Ethan the Ezrahite in the face of disaster, confirming God's faithfulness and the solidity of His covenant with them.]

The passage above says so much about our God. He loves His chosen ones and will never remove that love or betray His faithfulness. It may seem now at times, as it did in the psalmist's day, that God has turned from us, but His love remains true and steadfast. For God to abandon us would mar His own character. This will never happen.

God established a covenant with David—He devised it, He drew it up, and He voluntarily entered into it, David's lineage in the person of Jesus would continue on for eternity, and God swore by Himself placing His name on the line as collateral.

If God were to revoke His word, it would not only cast a shadow on His holiness but also contradict His perfection. Since God cannot lie, we know God's Word is true, and Jesus will reign forever! When God gives us a promise, we can rest assured it will be kept. Fruition may not come quickly…it may take years to develop, but He will see to it that His promises are fulfilled, because He is trustworthy, and His Word is solid.

Today, if you feel as if God is nowhere to be found, realize that His love remains; He will not betray His faithfulness to you; and whatever He whispered to you in those quiet places, He will bring about in His time. He is a Promise Keeper!

WHAT PROMISES HAS GOD MADE TO YOU? DO YOU BELIEVE HE WILL KEEP THEM?

DAY 90

PSALM 90:12

"Teach us to number our days, that we may gain a heart of wisdom."

~*~

[A psalm of Moses speaking about the brevity of life in comparison to the eternal nature of God.]

As a child, I heard older folks talk about how short life is; yet when you are seven or ten or even sixteen, life seems to go by at a snail's pace.

In today's verse, the psalmist petitions God to, "Teach us to number our days." This earthly life does not last forever and foolish is the one who is so consumed in the here-and-now without contemplating what lies beyond.

Matthew Henry writes, "We must live under a constant apprehension of the shortness and uncertainty of life and the near approach of death and eternity. We must so number our days as to compare our work with them, and mind it accordingly with a double diligence, as those that have no time to trifle."[6]

---

[6] "Matthew Henry Commentary-Psalms 90:12,"

None of us are guaranteed a long, prosperous life. At any moment, our number could be called up, and what we did with Jesus in this lifetime determines our eternity. Likewise, wisdom is understanding the brevity of life and placing total trust in the One who knows our beginning and end, our past and our future. **HOW DO YOU MAKE THE MOST OF THE LIFE GOD HAS GIVEN YOU?**

Matthew Henry, https://bible.prayerrequest.com/5000004-matthew-henry-commentary/psalms/90/12/90/12/.

DAY 91

PSALM 91:4-7

"He will cover you with his feathers, and under his wings you will find refuge; his faithfulness will be your shield and rampart. You will not fear the terror of night, nor the arrow that flies by day, nor the pestilence that stalks in the darkness, nor the plague that destroys at midday. A thousand may fall at your side, ten thousand at your right hand, but it will not come near you."

~*~

[We do not know the writer for certain. This is a beautiful testimony of those who trust in God.]

I love this psalm. Psalm 91 brings me to tears as I reflect on God's goodness towards His children.

Like a mother hen, God nestles us under His mighty wings and keeps us safe, warm, and dry. We have no reason to fear worldly terrors because He is in control and always on duty.

The psalmist says this about God's love in verse 14, "Because he loves me...I will protect him, for he acknowledges my name."

God is with you. God is with us. His love knows no boundaries, and He walks close beside those who walk with Him. To do anything other would be to abandon His character. Around us, we will see many fall away from the faith for various causes, but for those who keep their eyes on God, He will also keep their feet steadfast.

Spurgeon says, "Whole nations are infected, yet the man who communes with God is not affected by the contagion; he holds the truth when falsehood is all the fashion. Professors all around him are plague smitten, the church is wasted, the very life of religion decays, but in the same place and time, in fellowship with God, the believer renews his youth, and his soul knows no sickness."[7]

Today, may we stay close to God, our Father. May we not stray from the shelter of His love, for in Him is true freedom, peace, and safety.

HAVE YOU EVER HAD AN EXPERIENCE WHEN YOU SENSED GOD HOVERING AROUND YOU?

---

[7] "Blue Letter Bible: Psalm 91," C.H. Spurgeon, https://www.blueletterbible.org/Comm/spurgeon_charles/tod/ps091.cfm.

DAY 92

"They will still bear fruit in old age, they will stay fresh and green, proclaiming, "The LORD is upright; he is my Rock, and there is no wickedness in him."

~*~

[Chapter 92 was a song for the Sabbath day, a song of rest. Again, the author is unmentioned.]

I always pray before I study and have my daily quiet time, and on my birthday, I asked God to give me a special verse to speak directly to me. He did. The above-mentioned is a reminder of His continual presence as years and birthdays pursue, and in turn, an encouragement to continuously sing of His praises.

As we age the body begins to change and wear down. Don't we know it! Yet, even in that season of life when our strength may be waning, our mind may not be as strong, our hands a little shakier and a bit feebler, God is with us!

He promises the righteous that in those moments *He* will be their source of strength. *He* will be their comfort and peace. *He* will refresh their tired spirit and reward their days of service and loyalty. These dear,

189

weathered saints to which this psalm refers will proclaim the Lord's goodness and His love for them. They will not turn away but be even more resolved that He is their God and King.

So, here is to more birthdays and to God's faithfulness. "He is my rock and there is no wickedness in him."

DO YOU BELIEVE WE EVER REACH AN AGE WHEN GOD ALLOWS US TO RETIRE FROM SERVING?

DAY 93

PSALM 93:1-2

"The LORD reigns, he is robed in majesty; the LORD is robed in majesty and armed with strength; indeed, the world is firmly established, it cannot be moved. Your throne was established long ago; you are from all eternity."

~*~

[There is no title or author mentioned, but it is a psalm of God's sovereignty over all creation. What more can be said?]

The Lord reigns. End of story. He is in charge and still in control. Sometimes it seems as if the world is in chaos, and it is, but it is not due to God's lack of power or preeminence. We are given free will, and it is when we choose not to follow Him that we begin to see the ill effects of sin.

The Bible tells us that the Lord sits on His throne observing everything; hearing every word spoken; reading every thought. He is robed in all His majesty, and strength is His mighty arm. Kings, leaders, politicians, all of humankind will all come and go, but God will remain. He has always been and will always be, and there is coming a day when He will once again step out of heaven to come down not as a lamb, but as a Judge and King.

Are you ready? Are we ready for that day? For those of us who believe, it will be a day of a long-awaited reset. Not the kind that world leaders imagine, but one in which sin is finally done away with; when the saints are vindicated, and all God's faithful people experience the glory and reward of eternity with our King in Glory! Hallelujah!

WHAT ARE SOME ADJECTIVES YOU WOULD USE TO DESCRIBE GOD'S REIGN AND MAJESTY?

DAY 94

PSALM 94:18-19

"When I said, 'My foot is slipping,' your love, O LORD, supported me. When anxiety was great within me, your consolation brought joy to my soul."

~*~

[Psalm 94 is an appeal to God regarding the oppression of wicked rulers, but with the ultimate belief God will have the last say.]

The psalmist had come to a point where he felt he could not go on. This was it. What was happening around him was too much, and it was taking him under. But then, at his moment of greatest weakness and anxiety, the Lord stepped in and lifted him up, providing a way out.

Many countries are in a time of great turmoil. Ungodly leaders run amok wreaking havoc with people's lives, and sometimes it can seem as if the entire system will collapse.

Yet, what we can be sure of, is that God knows what is going on. He is well acquainted with those who are calling the shots. He hears their schemes and sees their evil deeds, and He is keeping a record of all their wicked moves.

At some point, when this time of judgment or testing is over, He will step in and bring relief to the oppressed. He will silence the foes and bind up the wounds of the hurting. God never forsakes His people, but He *does* allow them to make choices, and sometimes those choices bring unpleasant consequences. Thankfully, His love is unending, and He has not left us without hope.

DO YOU EVER FIND YOURSELF HAVING ANXIOUS THOUGHTS OVER WHAT IS GOING ON AROUND THE WORLD? WHAT DO YOU DO TO HELP HARNESS THOSE THOUGHTS?

DAY 95

"Come, let us bow down in worship, let us kneel before the LORD our Maker; for he is our God and we are the people of his pasture, the flock under his care. Today, if you hear his voice, do not harden your hearts as you did at Meribah..."

~*~

[A psalm most likely written by David (Hebrews 4:7) to both exhort and warn the Jewish people.]

I remember as a child and throughout my teen years, having moments when I would swear someone had spoken my name. I would turn around and see no one. After finally surrendering my life to Christ in my mid-twenties, those quiet whispers ceased. Whether God had actually called my name or I was hearing things, the fact of the matter remains: God will do what it takes to get our attention, and when He calls, we must listen.

In this psalm, the writer calls the people to gather for worship in humble submission to the Lord who is the Maker and Creator of all. They belong to Him and reside in His pastureland.

Likewise, we belong to God, and nothing we have

can be attributed to our own doing. Everything belongs to Him. We are just participants in this temporary temporal life.

The psalmist warns people not to harden their hearts but to God's calling. He goes on to illustrate how their ancestors resisted God's voice, which led to their wandering in the wilderness for forty years and missing out on the blessings of the Promised Land.

When God calls us, may we not harden our hearts and dull our ears to His prodding lest we miss out on the great blessings He has in store.

TODAY, HOW CAN YOU LISTEN BETTER FOR GOD'S STILL, SMALL VOICE?

DAY 96

"Declare his glory among the nations, his marvelous deeds among all peoples."

~*~

[This psalm is thought to be part of David's song when the Ark Of The Covenant was brought into the tent made to house it. It is a song of praise.]

God is King! Great news, right? For believers, it is our commission to go and tell this glorious message, not hide it away for ourselves. Likewise, before Jesus left this earth, He gave these instructions:

"Therefore, go and make disciples of all nations, baptizing them in the name of the Father and of the Son and of the Holy Spirit, and teaching them to obey everything I have commanded you. And surely, I am with you always, to the very end of the age (Matthew 28:19-20)."

We are to go and tell; to declare what the Lord has done. Yet, how many of us are silent when it comes to the Gospel? We will talk about the weather, the game, the latest movie, our neighbor, but not our Lord because we do not want to offend.

Yet, none of those other things will save. Nothing else can heal the hurts, bind the wounds, forgive the sins, change the hearts, or bring eternal salvation. Only God can do that, so we need to bring the message of hope to everyone!

Today, do not ignore an opportunity to tell someone what God has done. It may be exactly what they are dying to hear.

WHEN IS THE LAST TIME YOU TALKED TO SOMEONE ABOUT JESUS?

DAY 97

PSALM 97:10

"Let those who love the Lord hate evil, for he guards the lives of his faithful ones and delivers them from the hand of the wicked."

~*~

[No writer's name is mentioned, but this psalm is rejoicing in God's almighty power and reign in the world, and hints at the work of the Holy Spirit within its context.]

Believers, we are to hate evil not comply with it. Events in the here-and-now that are contrary to God's holy character and commands should turn our stomachs and cause us to long even more for our home which is not of this world. We should be reminded that God still reigns. So, in this chosen verse we are told "he guards the lives of his faithful ones and delivers them from the hand of the wicked."

This does not mean we will never encounter evil. We are in this world; therefore, we will experience hard things. It is certain that each of us will walk through the fire, but if we put our trust in God, He will preserve our soul. No man nor demon from hell can steal or destroy a soul which has been surrendered to the Lord for safe keeping. No, that soul belongs to Him, and even Jesus said in John 10:28, "I give them eternal life, and they shall never perish; no one can snatch them out of my hand."

At our appointed time, God will deliver us from this sinking ship of a world. The Lord is not shaken by the level of wickedness we see but will return and display His hand of might! He is the Victor! The battle has already been won, but we must wait for Him to return and claim His inheritance. He will be back. So, look up! And may we say, Glory to God! He is worthy to be praised!

CAN YOU REMEMBER A TIME WHEN GOD PROTECTED YOU FROM THE EVIL ONE? WHAT HAPPENED?

DAY 98

PSALM 98:7-9

"Let the sea resound, and everything in it, the world, and all who live in it. Let the rivers clap their hands, let the mountains sing together for joy; let them sing before the LORD, for he comes to judge the earth. He will judge the world in righteousness and the peoples with equity."

~*~

[This psalm has no author ascribed to it, but it is, as Spurgeon says, a "Coronation Hymn," rejoicing in the fact the Messiah has conquered the nations and revealed His righteousness.]

In the chosen passage, the psalter gives human-like actions to God's creation. The sea resounds, the rivers clap their hands, the mountains sing. All creation is jubilantly praising God and welcoming the righteous reign of the Lord, for they have been under sin's curse from the beginning and now rejoice at their anticipated and beautiful release.

I am sure you can think of a time when you sat beside a roaring ocean, walked through a meadow with its grasses waving in the wind, hiked near a rivers edge, or sat in city park surrounded by grass and trees.

Nature has a way of reminding us there is more to what the eye beholds. It is as if they are offering praises to our heavenly Father through their melodic and rhythmical hums, swooshes, trickles, and roars.

The psalter, here, also tells us He—the Messiah—is coming to judge the earth; he will rightly deal with all wickedness and the people with uprightness. So, sound the trumpets! Shout for joy! For God "has remembered his love and his faithfulness to the house of Israel; all the ends of the earth have seen the salvation of our God (vs. 3)." And, so, we say, come Lord Jesus, come!

DO YOU HAVE A FAVORITE NATURE SPOT YOU LIKE TO GO AND REFRESH YOUR THOUGHTS? WHAT IS IT ABOUT THAT LOCATION THAT MAKES IT EASIER FOR YOU TO REJUVENATE YOUR SPIRIT?

DAY 99

PSALM 99:9

"Exalt the Lord our God and worship at his holy mountain,
for the Lord our God is holy."

~*~

[The theme of this psalm is God's holiness which is mentioned three times. It also declares God's righteous acts towards His people.]

God is holy. What does that mean? It means He is set apart; morally righteous and pure; utter perfection.

A.W. Tozer describes God's holiness this way: "God is not now any holier than He ever was. And He never was holier than now. He did not get His holiness from anyone nor from anywhere. He is Himself the Holiness. He is the All-Holy, the Holy One; He is holiness itself, beyond the power of thought to grasp or of word to express, beyond the power of all praise."8

---

8 "A.W. Tozer: Are You Amazed by the Holiness of God?," Andrew Hess, https://churchleaders.com/daily-buzz/280706-aw-tozer-amazed-god-holiness.html.

Why then would He expect anything less out of His people? He says in 1 Peter 1:15-16, "But just as he who called you is holy, so be holy in all you do; for it is written: 'Be holy, because I am holy.'"

Unfortunately, due to our sinful nature, we struggle to perfectly fulfill this directive this side of heaven. For even the great Apostle Paul wrestled with sin and described his actions by saying, "We know that the law is spiritual; but I am unspiritual, sold as a slave to sin. I do not understand what I do. For what I want to do I do not do, but what I hate I do (Romans 7:14-15)."

This is no excuse, however. Our ultimate goal is to be holy. We should strive to imitate the characteristics of our Lord and keep in step with His steps. Our goal should be to love as He loves and desire to worship Him because He is holy. This, friends, is our challenge for today. Be holy, for God is holy.

WHEN YOU HEAR THE WORD HOLY, WHAT THOUGHTS CONJURE UP IN YOUR MIND, AND WHY?

DAY 100

"Shout for joy to the LORD, all the earth. Worship the LORD with gladness; come before him with joyful songs. Know that the LORD is God. It is he who made us, and we are his; we are his people, the sheep of his pasture. Enter his gates with thanksgiving and his courts with praise; give thanks to him and praise his name. For the LORD is good and his love endures forever; his faithfulness continues through all generations."

~*~

[This is a short psalm...a call to praise our Heavenly Father.]

This psalm delivers a call to action. His people are to shout for joy; to worship; to come before Him with joyful songs and know we belong to Him; to be thankful, for He is good.

We have so much to praise Him for. Ahh, but so many times we allow our circumstances to dictate our heart. Thus, our outward reactions or inactions fail to reflect a heart of praise.

Even the psalmist in Psalm 42:11 asked, "Why are you downcast, O my soul? Why so disturbed within me? Put your hope in God for I will yet praise him, my Savior and my God."

We must detach ourselves from our present situation and fix to the truth of the eternal—He is good and worthy to be praised *always*.

So, today let us focus on what God has done. Let us count the ways He has been faithful and brought us through difficulties. We belong to Him, and His love and faithfulness to us endures forever. This is something to be thankful for!

WHAT DO YOU THINK IT MEANS WHEN IT SAYS THAT WE ARE SHEEP FROM HIS PASTURE?

DAY 101

PSALM 101:2B-3

"I will walk in my house with blameless heart. I will set before my eyes no vile thing. The deeds of faithless men I hate; they will not cling to me."

~*~

[A psalm of David. He is about to be crowned king and is resolving to walk uprightly and becoming of a man after God's own heart.]

David begins this psalm by laying out his character before God and the people he will serve. In verse 2b, he is talking about his actions in his own home. How can a man or woman of God lead others if they cannot rightly manage or live out their faith within their own four walls?

David, likewise, resolved to not entertain anything that might lead him astray. He knew his limitations, as should we know ours, and just as he decided he would not subject himself to any vile thing for one small glance or fleeting moment of participation, so too, should we be as careful.

We know from scripture David eventually stumbled in this. He let down his guard and fell headlong into sin. Yet, as we all stumble at some point, David's example is a good reminder of how easily entrapped we can become.

So, just as David did in these verses, we must make it a continual habit to choose uprightness. We must steer clear of those things which cause us to trip and tumble. We must hate the evil in this world but love the sinner as Christ loves us.

HAVE YOU PUT ANY PERSONAL BOUNDARIES IN PLACE TO KEEP YOUR FOOT FROM SLIPPING INTO TEMPTATION?

DAY 102

PSALM 102:25-28

"In the beginning you laid the foundations of the earth, and the heavens are the work of your hands. They will perish, but you remain; they will all wear out like a garment. Like clothing you will change them and they will be discarded. But you remain the same, and your years will never end. The children of your servants will live in your presence; their descendants will be established before you."

~*~

[No specific writer mentioned though various names have been debated. The psalmist is lamenting his own personal suffering, but also on a national level as well.]

We see in the above passage that God laid the foundation of the earth, therefore anything else He chooses to do, such as rebuilding Zion, would be relatively effortless to Him.

Further, this psalm hints to the end of times when God will reclaim and retire His creation. The old order of things will pass away, but God will remain the same. God never alters. Though times and seasons change and life as we know it moves forward, God is steadfast.

In Malachi 3:6 He says, "I the LORD do not change. So you, O descendants of Jacob, are not destroyed." Likewise, Hebrews 13:8 says, "Jesus Christ is the same yesterday and today and forever." And finally, Isaiah 40:8 says, "The grass withers and the flowers fall, but the word of our God stands forever."

God remains the same, yet you and I change daily and are being quickly ushered closer to our eternal position, whether with God in His glorious Heaven or in everlasting separation and darkness.

Two things we should take away from this passage: God never changes and even when things seem impossible, nothing is too hard for the Lord.

WHAT ARE SOME WAYS YOU HAVE NOTICED PEOPLE AND THINGS AROUND YOU CHANGING?

DAY 103

PSALM 103:8-12

"The LORD is compassionate and gracious, slow to anger, abounding in love. He will not always accuse, nor will he harbor his anger forever; he does not treat us as our sins deserve or repay us according to our iniquities. For as high as the heavens are above the earth, so great is his love for those who fear him; as far as the east is from the west, so far has he removed our transgressions from us."

~*~

[A psalm of David praising God for His great love and compassion toward His people.]

With this psalm I say, Amen! Though God is perfect, holy, and morally righteous, those of us over whom He reigns, fail Him time and again. Like sheep, we have all gone astray; yet, in His infinite mercy and love, His anger does not linger. His compassion takes hold, and His forgiveness flows free to the repentant sinner.

Oh, how this should speak to our hearts and cause us to treat others with temperance and care. It was us who deserved that punishment on the cross, but it was He who bore our sin and made a way for restoration.

His love knows no bounds. He removes our confessed sins and remembers them no more; a tremendous burden lifted off our shoulders, so we may move forward in freedom released from the chains which weighed down so heavily upon us.

We have much to be thankful for. God is a just God, but also One of love and tender compassion. He is the Great Shepherd who will leave the ninety-nine to find His wandering lamb, and for that, like David, I am eternally grateful.

WHAT WOULD YOU SAY IS ONE OF GOD'S GREATEST CHARACTERISTICS?

DAY 104

"He makes winds his messengers, flames of fire his servants."

~*~

[The writer of this psalm is thought to be David, as the language and prose is similar to the psalm directly before it. The Septuagint also gives credit to David.]

Psalm 104 offers a condensed history of God creating the heavens and the earth; the waters and mountains; all living creatures and their sustenance; sun, moon, and stars. But in verse 4, we see an oddly peculiar statement. "He makes winds his messengers, flames of fire his servants." Some translations use the word "angels" instead of winds, but regardless, what we see here is all created things are at God's disposal.

Like a wind that is unseen but felt, angels work to carry out God's plans in our lives. The fire can represent purification, holiness, or judgment, and like God, Who is Spirit, these messengers and servants work in the spiritual realm, though there are biblical instances of physical manifestations, such as we see in

Numbers 22:23.

This passage is a good reminder that God has angel armies to accomplish things about which we know nothing. He moves and works often unseen, but when it is part of His plan to reveal those workings, we are often grand witnesses to miracles or other mysterious movements of God.

HAVE YOU EVER HAD AN ENCOUNTER WITH AN ANGEL?

DAY 105

PSALM 105:4

"Look to the LORD and his strength; seek his face always."

~*~

[This psalm was written by David when the ark was carried up to the place prepared (1 Chronicles 16:7).]

Several years ago, I began journaling. I do not do it every day...not even every month. I write when I have a specific prayer request to keep track of, or those times when God surprises me with crazy, out-of-the-blue blessings. Those are the things I specifically want to remember. It is neat to go back through the years and see how God showed up; to read answers to things I thought were impossible; to see how strong and faithful He was and is.

David reminded the people from where their help came. He then gave an account of the history of how the descendants of Abraham were brought to the foreign land of Egypt, and how their needs were met due to Joseph's diligence and God's providence. David tells of the great leader Moses, who led the people out of Egypt and to the Promised Land; the miracles God did in their midst; the plunder He gave them.

It is a good thing to look back and remember all that God has done for us. Often, we get so wrapped up in the here-and-now that we forget the past and His great works on our behalf.

This passage reminds us to look to God, not our spouse, not our employer, not the government, not our bank account, not anyone or anything else, for it is GOD who is our strength. He is our help. He is our guide, and we should seek His face continually, not just when we are in need.

Today, look up but bend your knee, for God is all we need. He is our strength.

DO YOU EVER FIND THAT IT IS DIFFICULT TO WAIT ON GOD'S PROVIDENCE AND TIMING?

DAY 106

PSALM 106:44-45

"But he took note of their distress when he heard their cry; for their sake he remembered his covenant and out of his great love he relented."

~*~

[Psalm 106 is a recollection of Israel's past sins and God's grace. Probably written by David, as both the first and last two verses were David's words to Asaph when he brought up the ark, found in 1 Chronicles 16:34-36.]

"But." This simple word shows God pausing in His anger long enough to remember the covenant He made with His people.

Though God had led the Israelites out of Egypt and miraculously saved them from their captors; though He led them by a pillar of cloud by day and fire by night; though He provided manna from Heaven and water from the rock; though He healed their infirmaries, they still sinned against Him.

They complained and grumbled; were envious of Moses and Aaron; fashioned a golden calf to worship; despised the land promised to them; yoked themselves to idols and other false deities; sacrificed their children to demons. These people lost their way, however, God had mercy on them.

God had every right to wipe them off the map, but instead, He took note of their distress. Like an attentive mother, He heard their cries. He remembered the covenant He had made with Abraham that Abraham's seed would be as immeasurable as the stars or the sand on the seashore. Out of His great love, He relented.

We still have this same God today. He sees our waywardness. He knows our secret sins. He looks upon our divided heart, but still, He cares for and has unconditional love for us.

HAVE YOU EVER EXPERIENCED GOD'S GREAT GRACE AND MERCY AT A TIME YOU WERE SPIRITUALLY FAR FROM HIM?

DAY 107

PSALM 107:14-16

"He brought them out of darkness and the deepest gloom and broke away their chains. Let them give thanks to the LORD for his unfailing love and his wonderful deeds for men, for he breaks down gates of bronze and cuts through bars of iron."

~*~

[Psalm 107 is a song of thanksgiving for all the ways in which God has come to the aid of the people—those in exile, those in bondage or prison, those who were sick, those being tormented at sea, etc. God is there for all who call upon His name.]

In verses 14-16, the psalmist is talking about God delivering those in bondage or imprisonment. As one example, we know from Scripture that God, through an angel, physically released Peter from his prison shackles (Acts 12-16). God also breaks the chains of those who are in spiritual bondage.

Throughout time, men and women have been under the weight of such heavy darkness living lives of sinful and destructive choices, yet, at some holy moment, God miraculously rescues them from their spiritual chains. No bar or shackle of hell was or ever will be strong enough to hold back the power of God in a person's life. When God chooses to set a person free, they are free indeed!

Charles Spurgeon says, "The Lord's deliverances are of the most complete and triumphant kind, he neither leaves the soul in darkness nor in bonds, nor does he permit the powers of evil again to enthrall the liberated captive. What he does is done forever. Glory be to his name."[9]

Yes! Glory be to His Name! For those once slaves to sin who have called upon the Name of Jesus, are now set free! No longer are we prisoners in chains for He breaks *every* chain. Hallelujah! Praise the Lord!

DO YOU KNOW SOMEONE WHO IS STILL IN BONDAGE TO SIN? WHY NOT PRAY FOR THEIR DELIVERANCE RIGHT NOW?

---

[9] "The Treasury of David: Psalm 107," Charles H. Spurgeon, https://archive.spurgeon.org/treasury/ps107.php.

DAY 108

PSALM 108:1

"My heart is steadfast, O God; I will sing and make music with all my soul."

~*~

[Psalm 108 is written by David. It is a song of thankfulness and prayers for mercy.]

Have you ever had those God-moments when something you had been praying for finally happened? Or maybe an unexpected blessing presented itself in an almost miraculous way? Those are the times you want to shout from the rooftops! Hey everyone, look at what God just did!

Several years ago, our grandson who was around nine, at the time, was taken into the ER for pain in his lower intestinal area. After several tests had been run, the doctor informed our grandson's parents that he had a mass on his colon and would be transported to a bigger hospital in a neighboring city. We were devastated. It seemed as if the air was sucked right out of the room leaving us gasping for the next breath.

Over the course of the afternoon, our grandson went into emergency surgery and had a goose egg-sized tumor removed along with some of his colon. It was all I could do to sit still and not fall into a heap on the waiting room floor. After some time, however, we received word the tumor was benign. He would have no lasting effects from it or the procedure. Our faith had been tested, but we learned that no matter the outcome, God is faithful.

In the above passage, David was basically saying: My heart is steadfast. It is fixed and unmovable. Though I have cares and worldly troubles; though others around me stumble, I have positioned my loyalty and thoughts in You, Lord. And, because I have resolved not to be thrown off course, I will be joyful and make You known, singing Your praises through whatever faculties You have given me—my words, my music, my actions, my work, and/or my intellect. Nothing else or no one else holds the esteem and honor You hold; therefore, my life will continually radiate You.

So, are you like David? Do your words tell others that because of Jesus, it is well? May this be our prayer today.

DAY 109

"With my mouth I will greatly extol the LORD; in the great throng I will praise him. For he stands at the right hand of the needy one, to save their life from those who condemn him."

~*~

[A psalm of David - a plea for help from the wicked.]

Junior High was a difficult time for me. I was new to the community, painfully shy, and an easy target for pranksters. I remember one day as I walked down the hallway, an older "mean" girl and her entourage decided it would be great fun to pull my skirt up in front of a hall full of kids. I was devastated…embarrassed…mortified. Yet, even in the midst of bullying episodes such as this one (and there were others), I had been given a firm foundation via my parents. I knew just how much I was loved and cherished by them and my Heavenly Father.

David was ready to praise the Lord before all mankind. For even during times of slander, mistreatment, and oppression, God never left David's side.

We also can know that we have a Great High Priest who understands the pain of those who have turned against us, for Jesus was betrayed by one from His own inner circle.

Yet here is the thing…Jesus saves. He was betrayed so we can live. He took the scorn and the shame upon Himself; therefore, we are set free from all condemnation. Even when we do suffer harassment in this life, Jesus is our greatest ally. He remains when all others fail us, and He gives us steady feet and an undying hope. That is something to praise!

JESUS NEVER LEAVES YOUR SIDE EVEN WHEN YOU GO THROUGH TRIALS. PRAY AND ASK FOR COMFORT AS YOU WORK THROUGH PROBLEMS AND ISSUES.

DAY 110

"The LORD says to my Lord: 'Sit at my right hand until I make your enemies a footstool for your feet.'"

~*~

[A psalm of David concerning the Messiah and His prophetical, priestly, and kingly rule]

Jehovah God is addressing Jesus Messiah about a time still yet to come but drawing nearer. To sit is a posture of rest but also a reflection of rule. Jesus' mission now complete, places Him in the position at God's right hand. He waits in peaceful anticipation for the culmination of God's ultimate plan to be fulfilled.

What a vision! Jesus, waiting patiently until God's appointed time. Why do you and I worry and fret when things don't happen right when we think they should? Wouldn't it make more sense for us to pattern our lives after Jesus Who is content in waiting for the perfect time?

David perceived that a day was set in motion when all the foes of Christ and His church would be put under the Messiah's holy and sovereign rule. When the last enemy is destroyed, the Kingdom will have been completely delivered to God the Father for the glory of the Son. These wicked people and nations of contempt will become the footstool the Great Messiah rests His feet upon, and His eternal reign will commence!

Many, in the fleeting moment of today, take great pleasure in sin and wickedness without thought of a day of reckoning, yet there is an appointed day coming when Jesus will stand up and reclaim what is rightfully His. As an old song lyric stated, "People get ready." He's coming back soon!

DO YOU LOOK FORWARD TO CHRIST'S RETURN? HOW ARE YOU PREPARING FOR THAT DAY?

DAY 111

"The works of his hands are faithful and just; all his precepts are trustworthy."

~*~

[An alphabetical (Hebrew) song of praise. The writer is not mentioned.]

As a child, I knew that my loving, but imperfect, parents had my best interests at heart. They were trustworthy, and I could depend on them to be there when I needed; to provide for all my needs, and give me sound biblical guidance in situations I faced as I grew. Yet, how much more dependable is our heavenly Father?

All God does is trustworthy and true. He shows no partiality or favoritism to His creation. The works of His hand display perfection. No wonder the psalmist offers continual praise! For we have no other who it can be said of the same.

The Apostle Paul wrote in Romans 8:28, "And we know that in all things God works for the good of those who love him, who have been called according to his purpose." This simply means God is always working out the situations we face, for our good.

First and foremost, He desires we have a relationship with Him, and He uses many ways, people, and circumstances, to help us realize our need for a Savior. Second, He uses every-day occurrences to make us more Christ-like. Those hard to love people, well, they are there to sand off the rough edges of our heart. That financial difficulty, it might be placed there to help you depend on Him and not your own provisions.

Likewise, God's commands are given for our protection and ultimate good. No flaws are found within them, and they are worthy of our obedience. Though some may falsely believe God's demands for righteous living are too heavy a burden, in reality, His ways are life-giving and freedom making, for He is the ultimate Designer, Creator and King!

As the Psalmist declares, may we praise the Lord, for to Him belongs eternal praise!

WHAT CIRCUMSTANCES HAS GOD USED IN YOUR LIFE TO DRAW YOU CLOSER TO HIM?

DAY 112

"He will have no fear of bad news; his heart is steadfast, trusting in the LORD."

~*~

[A comparison between the blessings of a righteous man and the fate of a godless man. This psalm coincides with the previous psalm in structure and presentation.]

In this psalm there are references to situations happening around the righteous person, which are out of his control, such as darkness (death, misery, sorrow), bad news, and fear; yet, because of the person's faith in God, he will not be shaken. Why? Because his heart is steadfast. Meaning the righteous person of God has fixed his gaze on the Lord. The righteous person has found great delight in God's commands, and He is faithful to walk them through whatever it is they face.

The person's heart has been transformed through a relationship with the Father, and despite the circumstances, he now find himself having more compassion and grace; are more generous towards others; has a good name to represent them; and he understands position [in Christ] is secure.

If we have entered into a commitment with Jesus, then we do not have to fear. There is no reason to be shaken anymore because we know He will take care of us no matter what.

HAVE YOU PLACED YOUR TRUST IN HIM?

DAY 113

"The LORD is exalted over all the nations, his glory above the heavens. Who is like the LORD our God, the One who sits enthroned on high, who stoops down to look on the heavens and the earth? He raises the poor from the dust and lifts the needy from the ash heap; he seats them with princes, with the princes of their people. He settles the barren woman in her home as a happy mother of children.

~*~

[A psalm of praise, possibly written for the temple liturgy.]

Recently, I watched a very touching documentary about orphan children in China. The show followed three different families who had adopted Chinese baby girls, and followed them throughout their growing up years, until they decided for themselves whether to return and seek their birth parents. For many orphan children, parents live in poverty and cannot feed another mouth. For others, they are abandoned and unwanted. Not with God, however. He sees our lowly state and has compassion. For these three girls, they were placed into the arms of barren women, and their lives were forever changed.

In the above section of Scripture, we see God in action. Here He sits enthroned; stoops down to look; raises up the poor and needy; settles the barren woman in her home and enables her to conceive. He does all these things and so much more!

God is always at work on our behalf, yet our enemy wants us to believe He has forgotten us or knows nothing of our sufferings. Listen, friend, nothing is farther from the truth. Our God is personally involved in each of our lives, and He will see to completion the plans He has for us.

Today, fix your gaze on Him. Keep a journal of those struggles you wrestle with. Pray daily, hourly, if need be, then step out of His way and see how He answers. He will. In time you will see.

HAVE YOU EVER KNOWN ANYONE WHO HAS ADOPTED OR BEEN ADOPTED? WHAT WAS THAT EXPERIENCE LIKE?

DAY 114

"When Israel came out of Egypt, the house of Jacob from a people of foreign tongue, Judah became God's sanctuary, Israel his dominion. The sea looked and fled, the Jordan turned back; the mountains skipped like rams, the hills like lambs. Why was it, O sea, that you fled, O Jordan, that you turned back, you mountains, that you skipped like rams, you hills, like lambs? Tremble, O earth, at the presence of the Lord, at the presence of the God of Jacob, who turned the rock into a pool, the hard rock into springs of water."

~*~

[A song of celebration for how God brought the people out of Egypt.]

Israel and his sons had gone down to Egypt as a family, and after years of slavery, brought out as a nation. The time they had toiled under harsh rule in a foreign land was over because God had heard their cries for help.

Often, God performed miracles when the way seemed hopeless. He parted the Red Sea for the Israelites' safe escape and held back the waters of the

Jordan River for their crossing. And when God descended upon the mountain to give Moses the law, it shook and trembled, for God's presence was too great. Nothing is too difficult or looming for God. For He is the Creator of all, therefore everything must bend a knee in submission.

This story of the Exodus also reflects what God did for sinners. He sent His Son, Jesus, down to "Egypt" where we were under the heavy burden and weight of our unrighteousness.

Jesus made the way through His death on the cross for us to be set free from that which entrapped us. When He led you and me out, we became part of a body of believers who will live with Him forever in Heaven. Therefore, we have much to celebrate!

WHAT IMPOSSIBLE SITUATION HAS GOD TURNED AROUND FOR YOUR GOOD?

DAY 115

"Not to us, O Lord, not to us, but to your name be the glory, because of your love and faithfulness!"

~*~

[A song sung at Passover - The psalmist petitions God to defend His name; describes false gods and those who worship them; exhorts the faithful to trust in God to work on their behalf; and describes how the dead cannot praise God but the people will.]

"Not to us...but to your name be the glory."

Whatever successes we have, whatever money in the bank, whatever land title we hold or in position we serve, these things do not come from us but from the hand of the Lord.

We often forget, as did the people in days of old, that it is not by our might we gain success. We are just a vessel God uses to accomplish His work. Any advancement or following is given by the Lord, for just as He gives, He can take away.

Theologian Matthew Henry says this, "...whatever good is wrought in us, or wrought for us, it is for His mercy and His truth's sake, because He will glorify his mercy and fulfil His promise. All our crowns must be cast at the feet of Him that sits upon the throne, for that is the proper place for them."[10]

Today, let us remember to give Him glory for who we are, what we can do, and what we have been given, for He is worthy. Glory to His name!

WHAT ARE SOME WAYS YOU CAN GLORIFY GOD THIS WEEK?

---

[10] "Verse-by-Verse Bible Commentary: Psalms 115:3," Matthew Henry, https://www.studylight.org/commentary/psalms/115-3.html.

DAY 116

PSALM 116:15

"Precious in the sight of the LORD is the death of his saints."

~*~

[Matthew Henry applies this psalm to David, however no name is mentioned. Regardless, it is a psalm of thanksgiving and praise for the Lord's great love and acts towards His people.]

Precious. That word means glorious, highly valued, rare, and influential. When the psalmist describes the death of one of God's servants as precious, we can know he means:

1. The person's death is glorious. Not that the act of dying nor the sin which introduced death into this world is glorious, but that he or she who has walked with God in their earthly life, are now entering their eternal home with never ending celebration and worship.

2. Second, God views the death of His servant as highly valued because his or her life was highly valued.

3. God is close to His children in their final moments. He brings them comfort and sees to it that they are carried safely to their heavenly home. Death has no hold on the one who is saved.

4. Finally, the deaths of those who have lived a life of humble service to God are influential. Many people have stood by the bedside of those who have loved Jesus well, only to hear their final pleas for their family to follow Him. A saint's death is influential not only in what they may say, but how they lived.

Charles Spurgeon says this, "The Lord watches over their dying beds, smooths their pillows, sustains their hearts, and receives their souls. Those who are redeemed with precious blood are so dear to God that even their deaths are precious to him. The deathbeds of saints are very precious to the church, she often learns much from them; they are very precious to all believers, who delight to treasure up the last words of the departed; but they are most of all precious to the Lord Jehovah himself, who views the triumphant deaths of his gracious ones with sacred delight. If we have walked before him in the land of the living, we need not fear to die before him when the hour of our departure is at hand."[11]

Precious. That's how God views the death of one of His saints, and that is how we can remember it.

HAVE YOU HAD SOMEONE PRECIOUS TO YOU PASS

---

[11] "The Treasury of David: Psalm 116," Charles H. Spurgeon,
http://www.romans45.org/spurgeon/treasury/ps116a.htm.

AWAY? HOW WOULD YOU DESCRIBE THEIR LIFE? HOW DID/DOES THIS AFFECT YOUR LIFE?

DAY 117

"Praise the LORD, all you nations; extol him, all you peoples. For great is his love toward us, and the faithfulness of the LORD endures forever. Praise the LORD."

~*~

[A short song sung as possibly a doxology or commencement of a passage. It is also the shortest chapter and thought to be the most middle section of the Bible.]

The psalmist calls upon all nations—all people including Gentiles, to praise God. We know from Romans 15:7-12, that God did not intend to only accept the Jews as His chosen people but would graft in the Gentile nations through the work of His Son to fulfill the promise He made to Abraham.

New Testament believers such as Peter, had a difficult time understanding God loved and died for all, and it took a vision straight from the Lord, Himself, to change this stubborn Apostle's mind. However, Peter, and many others, would come to embrace the fact all who accepted the free gift of eternal life Jesus bought with His own blood, would share in the eternal rewards God had promised.

The Bible tells us God's love is so great and His faithfulness so profound, that while we were yet sinners, Christ died for us *all*. (Romans 5:8). This is the great Gospel message; therefore, we have much to praise Him for.

HOW ARE YOU PRAISING GOD TODAY THROUGH YOUR LIFE...YOUR WORDS...YOUR ACTIONS? MAY WE ALL STOP AND REFLECT THE GOODNESS OF GOD AND, ESPECIALLY, NOT KEEP IT TO OURSELVES!

DAY 118

PSALM 118:24

"This is the day the LORD has made; let us rejoice and be glad in it."

~*~

[A psalm most likely written by David when at last he received the Kingdom to which he was anointed. This psalm also holds some prophetic verses pointing to Jesus, the awaited Messiah.]

This was a day of rejoicing! A new day and new era dawning as David took his rightful place as king. There was much celebration, music, and feasting going on in Jerusalem.

That moment, however great as it was, pales in comparison to the day to worship our Lord. The Sabbath day is the most important day of the week as we reflect upon all He has done for humankind; therefore, we should rejoice in it, and more importantly, in Him.

We also look forward to a day coming, when Jesus will return with both justice and mercy for all the world.

Today as you and I go about our daily tasks, may

we remember to find joy in this day we have been given. He has made it and we should rejoice in the fact we are still here, He has work for us to accomplish on His behalf.

DO YOU FIND IT EASY TO REJOICE IN EACH NEW DAY, OR DO YOU ALLOW TRIALS AND FRUSTRATIONS TO GET IN THE WAY?

DAY 119

"Your word is a lamp to my feet, a light for my path."

~*~

[This psalm is the longest of all Psalms. It is broken down into 22 sections, 8 verses each, with each section representing and starting with one of the letters of the Hebrew alphabet. Example: Aleph, Beth, Gimel, etc. Commentators of old ascribe this work to David, however there is some debate. The focus of this lengthy song is God's Word.]

A lamp and a light. What use are those things? To illuminate and to guide. Imagine walking down a dark road or a completely blackened hallway. Without some sort of light, a person might fall into a ditch or stumble over a rug. The same is with us. We are daily walking through this darkened world where there are pitfalls all around, and if we are not careful, we will fall right in.

God's Word is the light we need. It shines on our path giving us wisdom and discernment. It helps us decipher which is the best way or choice, but it also convicts us when we have made wrong turns. It offers us hope by pointing us to the One who holds our past and our future.

Being in God's Word daily is crucial for our survival amongst the wolves of this world. The psalmist describes it as giving light, peace, understanding, deliverance, comfort, and life. Therefore, I urge you...I plead with you...pick up the Bible. Read it for yourself. Learn from it. It is your roadmap to the next eternal life.

HOW HAS GOD'S WORD BEEN A LIGHT TO YOUR PATH?

DAY 120

PSALM 120:6-7

"Too long have I lived among those who hate peace. I am a man of peace, but when I speak, they are for war."

~*~

[The first song of fifteen ascents was possibly sung by those going up the steps from the outward court of the temple to the inward; also thought to be attributed to the stages of a journey. Commentators of old attribute it to David as he reflected back on his enemy Doeg.]

This first psalm is about individuals who slander in an attempt to destroy another person's character. The psalmist is a man of peace. If David is the writer, he was most likely reflecting back with fondness on the days when he was out in the fields with just his flock, no other responsibilities or status to put him in the line of criticism and hatred.

He had been among these peace haters too long. Their temperaments clashed, for night and day have nothing in common, yet, he had been compelled to remain.

Sometimes we, too, find ourselves in situations

with those who seem to look constantly for ways to create unrest. All you or I long for is peace, yet peace is not what they seek. So, what do we do? As the psalmist states in verse 1, "I call on the LORD in my distress, and he answers me." When we cannot talk to any other, we can talk to God. When no one else can be trusted to divulge our heart, God stands ready to listen and come to our aid.

The psalmist knew he could trust God to take care of the situation, and eventually, the one who had caused so much grief and heartache would be dealt with.

Know today that you are not alone. God sees you and knows how much you want peace. Run to and allow Him to vindicate and direct your steps.

HAVE YOU EVER HAD TO BE THE PEACEMAKER IN A SITUATION? HOW DID YOU FEEL?

DAY 121

PSALM 121:1-2

"I lift up my eyes to the hills— where does my help come from? My help comes from the LORD, the Maker of heaven and earth."

~*~

[So different from the first song of ascent, this psalm focuses on the peace and care of God.]

I lift *up* my eyes. True help cannot be found around or beside a person. Only when we lift our eyes to the One who sits on His heavenly throne, can we find real answers and assistance.

In this verse, the psalmist was possibly referring to Jerusalem or Mount Zion itself where the temple was located, and God's Presence dwelt. He recognized that no one or nothing could bring him the help he desired. Only God could, and so, we too must look up.

Spurgeon reminds us of God's great help with these words, "...let us lift up our eyes with hope, expectance, desire, and confidence. Satan will endeavor to keep our eyes upon our sorrows that we may be disquieted and discouraged; be it ours firmly to resolve that we will look out and look up, for there is good cheer for the eyes, and they that lift up their eyes to the eternal hills shall soon have their hearts lifted up also."[12]

Today when you sense your foot slipping or find yourself in need of help, lift your gaze. Your Maker is ready to assist and come to your aid. All you have to do is look up.

DOES KNOWING GOD IS YOUR HELP GIVE YOU PEACE IN TROUBLING TIMES?

---

[12] "C.H. Spurgeon: Treasury of David," C.H. Spurgeon, https://www.blueletterbible.org/Comm/spurgeon_charles/tod/ps121.cfm.

DAY 122

PSALM 122:1

"I rejoiced with those who said to me, 'Let us go to the house of the LORD.'"

~*~

[A third psalm of ascent written by David, for the people as they went up to celebrate the holy feasts in Jerusalem.]

In this verse, David is expressing his delight not only about going up to the house of the Lord for worship, but others were mindful to invite him to go along.

It is God's will that we gather regularly together in worship. If we look to the words in Hebrews 10:24-25 we read, "And let us consider how we may spur one another on toward love and good deeds. Let us not give up meeting together, as some are in the habit of doing, but let us encourage one another—and all the more as you see the Day approaching."

Yet what do we see today? We see a growing amount of people failing to gather or failing to invite others to go with them to worship our Lord.

David counted it a joy, a delight, and a duty to

worship God in His house; to give Him the thanks and praise for all He has done. Are we so readily eager to praise God, or do we prefer the comfort, convenience, and safety of our home and other events?

Listen, friend, it is imperative we make time to worship with our fellow believers. It is crucial to invite others to join us, for it is God's will for us to set aside time to come into His Presence and offer Him our praise. David considered it a delight and so must we.

DO YOU ATTEND CHURCH REGULARLY? IF NOT, WHY NOT?

DAY 123

PSALM 123:1

"I lift up my eyes to you, to you whose throne is in heaven."

~*~

[This song of ascent is known as "the song of eyes". The psalmist knows where hope comes from; it is up at the throne of God, so that is where he directs his gaze.]

I am married to a man who was in law enforcement for over thirty-three years. Police officers are trained never to close their eyes or bow their head. They need to be scanning the crowds or area constantly for anything which might take them by surprise. Our prayer life is kind of like that as well. When we pray, though a bowed head is certainly a symbol of humility and submission, often it is useful to pray with our heads and eyes lifted with great anticipation and expectancy.

Within this first stanza, "I lift up my eyes," reminds us of the verse in Psalm 121:1 which says, "I will lift up my eyes to the hills—where does my help come from?"

Though God is everywhere, we naturally associate

252

Him with Heaven's throne room above the upper heavens. He is our promise of hope, strength, power, comfort, etc., so the psalmist calls out to Him believing He will step forth and defend His righteous ones.

Let me ask you, where does your help come from? Who do you turn to when faced with uncertainty? If you are like so many others who only rely on themselves or on the help of individuals, unfortunately that type of help will eventually come up short.

Yet, if you and I turn our gaze to Him believing He will step in and assist us in our time of need and trusting He has our best interests at heart, then surely our hope will be renewed, and we will experience God's beautiful grace in our life.

WHEN YOU PRAY, DO YOU LIFT YOUR EYES UP TOWARDS THE SKY?

DAY 124

PSALM 124:1-5

"If the LORD had not been on our side—let Israel say—if the LORD had not been on our side when men attacked us, when their anger flared against us, they would have swallowed us alive; the flood would have engulfed us, the torrent would have swept over us, the raging waters would have swept us away."

~*~

[David is most likely the author of this song of ascent. He is praising God for Israel's deliverance by God's mighty hand.]

There is a popular Christian artist who wrote a song talking about some of the feelings she has felt in the lonely and desperate times of life; how she did not know who she would be if she did not have God in her life.

Unfortunately, because we live in a broken world, there are bound to be moments when we feel as if life is crashing down around us. For those of us who are believers, we know if it was not for God, we might just fall off the edge. Yet, thankfully, He holds us in His hands.

In this psalm, David is praising God for stepping in and saving Israel from their troubles.

Israel has always been a nation of turmoil, even though they are considered the apple of God's eye. Their enemies have been, and still are many, yet a remnant has always been spared by the Great hand of God because of His tender mercies.

This psalm also speaks to us today. Many of us have felt the flood and the rage and the waves against us. This world is not our home, and it can often be a harsh place filled with many disappointments and trials. However, like David, we must see through those hard times we have experienced, and say, "If it were not for God, I would not have made it."

CAN YOU THINK OF A TIME WHEN GOD SAVED YOU FROM A TERRIBLE ENDING? WHAT HAPPENED?

DAY 125

PSALM 125:1-2

"Those who trust in the LORD are like Mount Zion, which cannot be shaken but endures forever. As the mountains surround Jerusalem, so the LORD surrounds his people both now and forevermore."

~*~

[This song of ascent is descriptive of the care and protection God affords His people. The writer is unnamed.]

Jerusalem is located within a hilly or mountainous region. When the psalmist relates a person who puts their trust in God to Mt. Zion, like the natural topography of the land, he is displaying a fixed, unmovable position both now and eternally.

Mt. Zion and her immovable position can also refer to the church where the gates of hell will not and cannot prevail against it. It is fixed and not easily shaken because whatever God establishes cannot be undone.

Jesus reiterated this theme when He spoke to Peter in Matthew 16:18 saying, "And I tell you that you are Peter, and on this rock I will build my church, and all the gates of Hades will not overcome it."

You and I may be knocked down at times by the enemy and his tactics, but because of God's unfailing love and never-ending mercies, we will not be shaken off our solid foundation. Like Zion, we stand immovable.

ARE YOU EASILY SHAKEN OVER SITUATIONS OUT OF YOUR CONTROL? HOW DO YOU MANEUVER THOSE MOMENTS?

DAY 126

PSALM 126:1-6

"When the LORD brought back the captives to Zion, we were like men who dreamed. Our mouths were filled with laughter, our tongues with songs of joy. Then it was said among the nations, 'The LORD has done great things for them.' The LORD has done great things for us, and we are filled with joy. Restore our fortunes, O LORD like streams in the Negev. Those who sow in tears will reap with songs of joy. He who goes out weeping, carrying seed to sow, will return with songs of joy, carrying sheaves with him."

~*~

[Possibly written by Ezra, though he is not named. This psalm of ascent was written when the people were brought back out of exile.]

There is much rejoicing in this seventh song of ascent. The people have been in exile from their beloved homeland and have now returned. Because of their years of sorrow, they can much more easily understand the overwhelming joy of the Lord!

This is not unlike a person who has been under the grip of the enemy's demonic influence and submerged in all its darkness and sin, finally to be set free and cast forth into the land of God's glorious freedom and light. What an experience! What a joyful occasion!

A man or woman who has been set free from spiritual bondage desires nothing more than to help others find that same road of freedom. Therefore, they toil to share the good news, oftentimes with tears in their eyes. And, one day, their hard work will pay off.

At some point, God will bring a harvest from their fruitful labor. Those who have been prayed over and for; others who have had the gospel message proclaimed to them; and many who have witnessed the joy and peace in a believer's life will finally come and surrender to Christ's Lordship. They, too, will find release from their captivity. This is our hope and prayer.

TODAY, ON WHOM ARE YOU WAITING TO FIND SPIRITUAL FREEDOM? KEEP WAITING WITH HOPE AND ANTICIPATION. GOD WILL MAKE THE WAY.

Day 127

Psalm 127:1

"Unless the LORD builds the house, its builders labor in vain. Unless the LORD watches over the city, the watchmen stand guard in vain."

~*~

[This song of ascent was either penned by David for Solomon, or by Solomon himself. It is considered, as Spurgeon puts it, a "Builder's Psalm," for everything is built by God.]

Here we read that unless God builds a house, a family, a city, an empire, etc., it will be built in vain. Just as in biblical days when men tried to erect the Tower of Babel to reach to the sky, God was not in it, and so, He scattered them, leaving only a wasted shell of a monumental task.

Yet, when Solomon built God's holy temple, the Lord was the center of the building project, and He blessed Solomon's work, causing even pagans to help in its magnificent construction. This goes to show how any undertaking must be built by the Lord or it will eventually crumble and fall.

Likewise, when heads of nations place themselves

as ultimate authority; when leaders of churches become dictatorial; when business CEOs take credit for their successes; when armies put their trust in their own might and strength, etc., then they have set themselves up for utter failure.

This psalm teaches us God must be at the forefront of every home, every project, every house of worship, every government, and military, or else, the hand of God will come against, and its ruin will be sure to follow.

WHAT ARE YOU "BUILDING" TODAY? IS IT YOUR CAREER, A FAMILY, A HOME, ETC.? ARE YOU PLACING GOD FIRST? IF NOT, WHY NOT?

DAY 128

"Blessed are all who fear the LORD, who walk in his ways. You will eat the fruit of your labor; blessings and prosperity will be yours. Your wife will be like a fruitful vine within your house; your children will be like olive shoots around your table. Thus is the man blessed who fears the LORD."

~*~

[This song of ascent is considered a family hymn. No writer is mentioned.]

I have a friend who has seven children. Just knowing that detail alone makes her great (or crazy) in my eyes, but there is much more to her than being a mother. This woman radiates God's goodness. She is a pastor's wife who does not tire of teaching, helping, serving, and leading within their church and community. I've not asked her husband, but I assume he would agree she is a fruitful vine which God has used in so many different ways.

In this passage, the writer begins by saying, "Blessed are all who fear the LORD, who walk in His ways." He is stating their Heavenly Father provides for them, guides and loves them, and because they work as God intended, they reap a portion of their labor for their own satisfaction and enjoyment.

God created woman for man, so, the wife of a God-fearing man will be a fruitful vine to him. She will produce a bounty of love, compassion, kindness, and help for her husband.

Within this song of blessing, the writer also notes the gift of children who around a table are a joyous yet noisy event. He praises God for these gifts which God bestows, likening them to olive shoots arising from an older, mature branch.

And just as this song intended, we should rejoice in our family. Marriage, children, jobs, the love of a spouse, are all great blessings of God to us and we should readily thank Him for such.

WOULD YOUR SPOUSE CONSIDER YOU TO BE A FRUITFUL VINE?

DAY 129

"They have greatly oppressed me from my youth, but they have not gained the victory over me."

~*~

[This song of ascent was clearly written by someone advanced in years. No author is mentioned, however. It is a song about Israel's continued persecution.]

The writer of this song was looking back at all the years of oppression created by Israel's enemies, yet they had not succeeded in crushing Israel because the hand of the Lord was continually upon them.

We can apply this truth to our own life. The enemy has often sought to harass, tempt, trip up, and belittle us. But we followers of Christ know our adversary does not ultimately win this fight, for Christ is the Victor!

Though you and I may go through struggles and trials here on earth...some extremely hard or even horrible things, we can have confidence our hope remains with Jesus. He is the author of our faith (Hebrews 12:2).

Today, whether you are wrestling with a difficulty or life is going well, thank God for always defending you and giving [you] reasons to continue on. Without His great love and mercy, none of us could stand.

HOW HAS GOD SHOWN YOU HIS ULTIMATE VICTORY IN YOUR LIFE?

DAY 130

PSALM 130:3-4

"If you, O LORD, kept a record of sins, O LORD, who could stand? But with you there is forgiveness, therefore you are feared."

~*~

[This song of ascent seems like a continuum of the previous, however after much suffering, the writer of this song displays hope.]

I put a big ole dent down the side of my dad's beloved truck. I was sixteen or seventeen and had not had my license long. I drove over to my boyfriend's house, and as I backed out of his drive, I cut the wheel too sharp and ran right over the top of their mailbox...while the family stood outside waving their hands at me. First impressions (smile). I waited hours to tell my dad. A freshly ground-in scratch and dent down the side of his truck was more than I could bear. Yet, I gathered up the courage and explained to him what had happened. You know what he said? "I'm so glad you weren't hurt." He did not hang this sin over my head. Instead, my dad offered me complete forgiveness.

In verses 3 and 4 we find the basics of the gospel message: We have all sinned, are *all* guilty before a holy God (Romans 3:23), and it is those sins which separate us from Him.

On our own merit, we could not stand in His presence. You and I are in desperate need of forgiveness, and this can only come through one source—Jesus.

Verse 7 goes on to say, and talking about the Lord, "with him is full redemption." Christ offered Himself and paid the price for our sins fully (1 Peter 2:24). This reminds us of the old hymn words, "Jesus paid it all. All to Him I owe. Sin had left a crimson stain, He washed it white as snow."

Do you have a favorite Bible verse or song which talks about God's forgiveness of sins?

DAY 131

PSALM 131:1-3

*"My heart is not proud, O LORD, my eyes are not haughty;
I do not concern myself with great matters or things too
wonderful for me. But I have stilled and quieted my soul; like
a weaned child with its mother; like a weaned child is my
soul within me. O Israel, put your hope in the LORD both
now and forevermore."*

~*~

**[A song of ascents by David and about David. It
displays his humility and servant-like heart, content
in the place and position God has called him to.]**
This is such a beautiful, short psalm which gives
us a challenge to our own soul. As David did, we need
to humble ourselves and learn to be satisfied with
whatever position in life the Lord has placed us in.

Charles Spurgeon says this about David's humble
words, "...As a private man he did not usurp the
power of the king or devise plots against him: he
minded his own business, and left others to mind
theirs. As a thoughtful man he did not pry into things
unrevealed; he was not speculative, self-conceited, or
opinionated. As a secular person he did not thrust

himself into the priesthood as Saul had done before him, and as Uzziah did after him. It is well so to exercise ourselves unto godliness that we know our true sphere, and diligently keep to it."[13]

This may be a struggle for many, but with the help of the Lord, and the guidance of His holy Word, we can obtain a heart of humility and sacrifice. Ask God to begin a new work in your heart and remove the prideful lusts of the flesh. Serving Him in true humility puts us in position for grander things.

"The LORD sustains the humble but casts the wicked to the ground." - Psalms 147:6

HOW DO YOU GO ABOUT QUIETING YOUR SOUL?

---

[13] "The Treasury of David – Psalm 131," Charles H. Spurgeon, https://archive.spurgeon.org/treasury/ps131.php.

DAY 132

"O LORD, remember David and all the hardships he endured. He swore an oath to the LORD and made a vow to the Mighty One of Jacob: 'I will not enter my house or go to my bed—I will allow no sleep to my eyes, no slumber to my eyelids, till I find a place for the LORD, a dwelling for the Mighty One of Jacob.'"

~*~

[This song of ascent was possibly written by Solomon as he looked back on his father, David's desire to build a temple for the Lord, and God's covenant with David regarding his lineage throughout all generations.]

"O LORD, remember…"

There are times in a believer's life when we cry out to God and say, O Lord, remember me! Just like the thief on the cross who uttered to Jesus in Jesus' final moments, "…remember me when you come into your kingdom (Luke 23:42)." Or like Joseph who said to the king's cupbearer after interpreting his dream, "…remember me and show me kindness; mention me to Pharaoh and get me out of this prison (Genesis

40:14)."

We want to be remembered, especially when it comes to God. You and I desire Him to recall all the times we served diligently in order that those deeds be acknowledged and weighed in the balance.

In these first few verses, the psalmist was petitioning the Lord to remember His servant, David, and to not forget how David had fought for and longed to build a temple for the Lord.

David had been faithful to God and had served Him well. Though he experienced many hardships and trials, his main priority was to build a temple where the ark of the covenant—the mercy seat of God—could finally rest.

The good news for us is that God never forgets our love and service, and our standing with Him is not based on our own merit. Thankfully, our position hinges solely on whether we have a relationship with His Son, Jesus.

In David's case, God had already made a promise or covenant with David that his kingly lineage would continue and eventually usher in the Messiah. And, God never breaks a promise!

Today, we should examine our heart and see if we are relying more on the things we have done for God, or on our relationship *with* God. There is a huge difference between the two.

ARE YOU RELYING SOLELY ON YOUR GOOD DEEDS OR ON THE SACRIFICE OF JESUS?

DAY 133

PSALM 133:1

"How good and pleasant it is when God's people live together in unity!"

~*~

[This song of ascent written by David is all about unity amongst tribes, families, churches, and communities.]

Alistair Begg once wrote, "You will likely have heard the saying that sticks and stones can break our bones, but words can never harm us—but that is dead wrong. Bruises may fade and the marks they made be forgotten. But hurtful words that have been said to us and about us tend to remain with us for a long time."[14]

David knew this all too well. He was a man fairly acquainted with bickering and petty fighting, even within his own household. Thus, when he wrote this song, it was his purpose to describe the importance of unity amongst believers and describe the God-honoring beauty of people who overlook differences

---

[14] "Words that Harm," Alistair Begg, https://truthforlife.org/devotionals/alistair-begg/02/26/2022/.

and choose instead to find common ground.

We certainly can take lessons from this psalm. Imagine what message our families, church houses, or social media pages would send to a non-believing world if we were more careful with our words and less critical of others.

What if we chose to build others up instead of finding ways to tear them down? What picture would this paint of the God we serve?

Today, may our words be few, and may they be saturated in love, for when we treat others as our Father commands us to do, it is like a honeycomb to the lips.

IS THERE ANYONE YOU HAVE NOT OFFERED FORGIVENESS TO? WHY NOT EXTEND YOUR HAND TO THEM TODAY?

DAY 134

PSALM 134:1-3

"Praise the LORD, all you servants of the LORD who minister by night in the house of the LORD. Lift up your hands in the sanctuary and praise the LORD. May the LORD, the Maker of heaven and earth, bless you from Zion."

~*~

[The last of the song of ascents, this song challenged and encouraged those Levites who ministered in the Lord's house.]

No writer is mentioned with this psalm; however, the psalter is concluding the ascent with closing remarks, almost as a goodbye blessing to those who oversaw the temple. These words speak to ministers today who keep watch over those whom God has entrusted to them.

First, they are called to praise the Lord always. Ministers set the example for the rest of their people to follow, and God ordains and takes delight in praise.

Second, they are to praise Him even in the night watch when all has grown dark in the world and light is hard to come by. They are to offer encouragement and pray for those who are in their care.

Third, they are to lift their hands in the sanctuary. Every part of their person and service should extol the Lord. The Apostle Paul wrote to Timothy in 1 Timothy 2:8 these words, "I want men everywhere to lift up holy hands in prayer, without anger or disputing." Holy hands are what God seeks, as well as ministers with a pure heart and a humble position.

Finally, as the people begin their descent from the temple, the minister(s) offers up a blessing upon the people through song. What more could anyone desire than to know they have been prayed for? What more than to have petitions lifted on their behalf? This was surely an encouragement to the people as they descended.

May we not forget to pray for one another, and those who serve us in our houses of worship today.

IS YOUR PASTOR A MAN OF PRAYER? DO YOU PRAY FOR YOUR PASTOR REGULARLY? PASTORS ARE HUMAN AND CAN STRUGGLE WITH THEIR OWN SELFISH DESIRES. TODAY, WHY NOT SEND YOUR PASTOR AN ENCOURAGING NOTE AND LET HIM KNOW YOU ARE LIFTING HIM UP.

DAY 135

PSALM 135:15-18

"The idols of the nations are silver and gold, made by the hands of men. They have mouths, but cannot speak, eyes, but cannot see. They have ears, but cannot hear, nor is there breath in their mouths. Those who make them will be like them, and so will all who trust in them."

~*~

[This psalm is like a patchwork quilt with repetitious passages from many other verses within Psalms, Deuteronomy, Exodus, Jeremiah, etc., all combined. No writer is mentioned.]

In the above verses, the psalmist is talking about idols other people groups have formed and fashioned in their own image, yet no life is found within them. These idols, though worshipped, cannot hear, see, think, speak, or understand. They are simply objects created by human hands.

Isaiah 44:17-18 says, "From the rest he makes a god, his idol; he bows down to it and worships. He prays to it and says, "Save me; You are my god!" They know nothing, they understand nothing; their eyes are plastered over so they cannot see, and their minds closed so they cannot understand."

These verses do three main things: First, they show us all mankind desires something or someone to worship. We all long for that One bigger than we are, and people will go to great lengths to worship either something created, i.e., themselves, prosperity, another person, a created entity, etc., or the Creator, God.

Second, these verses display how foolish it is to worship useless idols hand-crafted by human hands, when we have a Creator God who is all-knowing, all-seeing, and all-powerful.

Third, the worship of anything besides the One true God is futile and ultimately destructive.

Today, you and I can get caught up in worshipping our careers, money, talents, our spouse or children, our 401k, social media outlets, whatever it may be, but what we need to recognize is until we lay those things down and put our total faith and trust in God alone, we will not have true inner peace from the Father. He does not and will not share His glory with another.

WHAT IS ONE THING GOD IS IMPRESSING UPON YOU TO SET ASIDE IN ORDER TO REFOCUS ON HIM? If you've made an idol of something, say this prayer, and commit to God being first in your life.

FATHER, PLEASE FORGIVE ME WHEN I PLACE OTHER THINGS BEFORE YOU; WHEN I MAKE IDOLS OUT OF THINGS OR PEOPLE WHO WILL NOT AND CANNOT AID OR OFFER THE SATISFACTION THAT YOU CAN. IN YOUR HOLY NAME, AMEN.

DAY 136

PSALM 136:1

"Give thanks to the LORD, for he is good. His love endures forever."

~*~

[A song of praise sung in Solomon's temple (2 Chronicles 7:3,6) for all God had done for Israel. This Psalm parallels 135, with much of the same verbiage.]

Throughout this song, the phrase, "His love endures forever," is sung after each verse. It is a solemn reminder God's love and mercy cannot be altered, turned off, redirected, or cancelled out. He loves us and nothing we can do or say will change the love He has.

Likewise, within this verse the psalmist calls the people to give thanks for He is good. In the dark times of our life, He is good. In the chaotic and uncertain moments, He is good. In the joyous and happy times, He is good. God is constant, and His character does not change.

In Psalm 34:8, David had encouraged the people with these words, "Taste and see that the LORD is good; blessed is the man who takes refuge in him."

David understood God is good, and everything He does or allows in our life is a reflection of His goodness. If you and I will try we can experience His goodness for ourselves; we will know, in fact, that God is looking out for our best interests.

HOW HAS GOD LOOKED OUT FOR YOUR BEST INTERESTS THIS WEEK? HE IS GOOD!

DAY 137

PSALM 137:4

"How can we sing the songs of the LORD while in a foreign land?"

~*~

[Chapter 137 is a song from one who was part of the exile to Babylon. The writer is lamenting over what was done to them and the sorrow they endured at the hands of their captors.]

Many people of God throughout time have been ravaged or displaced due to the wickedness of others. Israel was no exception. Due to their own waywardness and sinful choices, God allowed them to be captured and driven from their homeland.

Their enemies taunted the people by demanding they sing songs of worship to God as they had done long before their captivity. Not because their captors wanted the enjoyment of music, but for further mockery.

There is a lesson we can learn here. When we are in a foreign place—spiritually and emotionally—it is difficult to properly worship the Lord. Only when we have turned back to God and He has placed our enemies of distraction under our feet, are we readily able to again sing His praises, uninhibited and unrestrained.

Whatever has possibly sidelined you or caused a loss of spiritual focus in your life, cry out to God. Ask Him to bring you out of captivity and back into the freedom of worship. He will, and your heart will once again sing for joy.

HAS YOUR HEART BEEN IN A FOREIGN PLACE? WHAT STEPS CAN YOU TAKE TO RESET YOUR HEART?

DAY 138

PSALM 138:8

"The LORD will fulfill his purpose for me; your love, O LORD, endures forever; do not abandon the work of your hands."

~*~

[The writer is David. The message is one of praise for what God has done and what He will still do.]

As a young shepherd, David had been anointed for the position of king. Yet, much time has passed, and David's enemies have tried to stop this coronation from happening.

In this chapter, David is reflecting over all God had done for him, and also how David had worshipped and longed for others to worship the One true God. In doing so, he had confidence and faith that God would, at some point, fulfill His plan for David to be king.

No enemy, nor their futile attempts can stop a plan of God's from happening. If He has willed it, then He will see it through to completion because He is true to His character.

In our own lives, God has set into motion His plans for us, and has called us into certain areas of service. No matter what the enemy throws our way, if God desires it and we cooperate with Him, nothing can thwart His plans. It will happen when the time is right. So, friend, rest assured. He has not forgotten you, nor His calling upon your life. He will see it to completion.

WHAT PURPOSE DOES GOD HAVE FOR YOU TO DO?

DAY 139

PSALM 139:13-16

"For you created my inmost being; you knit me together in my mother's womb. I praise you because I am fearfully and wonderfully made; your works are wonderful, I know that full well. My frame was not hidden from you when I was made in the secret place, when I was woven together in the depths of the earth. Your eyes saw my unformed body; all the days ordained for me were written in your book before one of them came to be."

~*~

[One of the more popular psalms, this one describes the omniscience and omnipresence of God—His infinite knowledge of all things, even in the most remote or microscopic areas, as well as His ability to be everywhere simultaneously. That is our God!]

In this section of the psalm, David is describing God's active and creative hand in the forming of David in his mother's womb.

God is the Creator of all life. By His hand we are formed and fashioned into who He deems us to be. He knows what makes us tick but also how many days we have on this earth.

The enemy, that great deceiver, has tried to trick people, however, into believing life is disposable and sometimes an inconvenience, but how farther from the truth!

God creates people with purpose in mind. Every single person ever conceived had/has a purpose, a value. Each of us is uniquely formed by a loving Father, and are dearly loved by Him. Each life is sacred to God, therefore, life should be sacred to us.

Whenever you begin to doubt your worth, remember God chose you. He formed you with His own hands and made you. While who you are today, your personality and circumstance, may have been influenced by the world and the people in it, this world is not your maker. You did not come into existence by accident or human will. God created you with affection and purpose in mind. YOU are dearly loved and nothing about your existence is a mistake.

For those precious little ones who never got the opportunity to experience life outside the womb, we can rest assured per scripture, they are with Jesus, and are fully whole, fully well, and fully rejoicing at His feet.

IF YOU HAVE BIOLOGICAL CHILDREN, HOW WOULD YOU DESCRIBE THE MIRACLE OF THE LIFE YOU FELT WITHIN YOU? FOR ALL OTHER MOMS AND DADS, WHAT WERE YOUR THOUGHTS THE FIRST TIME YOU HELD YOUR CHILD IN YOUR ARMS?

DAY 140

PSALM 140:12-13

"I know that the LORD secures justice for the poor and upholds the cause of the needy. Surely the righteous will praise your name, and the upright will live before you."

~*~

[A psalm of David, petitioning God for deliverance from his enemies and justice for their deeds.]

A couple of years ago, my husband and I attended a Christian pop concert where packets were made available at the end of the night. These packets contained the picture, name, and information about a child in a third-world country who was looking for a sponsor. I had previously thought about "adopting" one of these kiddos, but had never been presented with the opportunity. Here was my chance. I grabbed a packet and ever since, have been helping my Ethiopian son to have access to education, good nutrition, health care and, of course, to hear the Gospel message

Often it is the poor and needy who get overlooked, neglected, and even worse, abused at the hands of the wealthy. It was certainly like that in Bible times, and is, unfortunately, not much different today.

Because these weaker people have no way of standing up to their more powerful foe, in this psalm, David is trusting God to step in and help those who cannot help themselves. His hope is when the day of judgment comes, those who seemingly had it all in this lifetime and misused their place of position, will realize their sinful actions towards others.

The final promise is when all is said and done in this life, God will bless those who humbly served Him and great will be their reward, but the wicked will be destroyed.

Today, when evil men seem to have the upper hand, remember God has the final say, and the Bible tells us the meek will inherit the earth (Matthew 5:5).

HAVE YOU HAD AN OPPORTUNITY TO HELP SOMEONE LESS FORTUNATE THAN YOU?

DAY 141

PSALM 141:3

"Set a guard over my mouth, O LORD; keep watch over the door of my lips."

~*~

[A psalm of David as he poured out his heart to God, His only friend. Everyone else, it seemed, had turned against him and were trying to trap David by his words.]

Once a word is spoken, it cannot be gathered back.

Whether good or bad, our words carry weight, and David was asking God to place a guard over his lips so he would not say anything the wicked could use against him.

Even the writer of Proverbs understood the importance of our words when he wrote, "Like an earring of gold or an ornament of fine gold is a wise man's rebuke to a listening ear (Proverbs 25:12)."

Jesus, too, warned the religious leaders about their words when he said, "You brood of vipers, how can you who are evil say anything good? For out of the overflow of the heart the mouth speaks (Matthew 12:34)."

I'm sure we have all been hurt by words, but we've also said words harmful or inappropriate. Today, may we speak only those things which are helpful and encouraging to others, and reflective of our relationship with the Lord. Father, set a trap over our lips and keep us from falling into evil with our words.

WHAT DO THE WORDS YOU SPEAK SAY ABOUT YOUR HEART?

DAY 142

PSALM 142:2

"I pour out my complaint before him; before him I tell my trouble."

~*~

[A prayer of deliverance from the hand of David's enemy, Saul, while hiding in a cave located in Engedi, Adullam, or some other location.]

David was a warrior; he was often pursued by those who sought his life. Numerous times he found himself fleeing and hiding so his enemies might not fulfill their evil plots against him.

In this verse, David has no one to turn to. He is in a damp, dark cave, not in a cushy palace. He is hiding from Saul, not boldly and openly sitting on his throne.

This is definitely not the ideal situation, yet instead of whining to, complaining about, or blaming others, he is crying out to God who hears and sees. David pours out his troubles to God, not because God does not know, but He desires David to come to Him for the solutions and for comfort.

ARE YOU EXPERIENCING SOMETHING DIFFICULT TODAY? INSTEAD OF SHARING IT ON SOCIAL MEDIA

OR WITH YOUR FRIEND OR SPOUSE, TAKE IT TO GOD FIRST. HE WANTS TO HELP YOU, AND BESIDES, HE IS THE ONE WITH ALL THE ANSWERS.

DAY 143

PSALM 143:8

"Let the morning bring me word of your unfailing love, for I have put my trust in you. Show me the way I should go, for to you I lift up my soul."

~*~

[Yet another psalm of David for vindication from his foes.]

How awesome it is to awaken in the morning hours to the realization of how much the Lord loves and cares for you. Likewise, how good it is to spend those early hours with Him in prayer and meditation on His Word. These are sacred moments which provide so much guidance and insight.

David was often chased and harassed by his enemies; however, the one constant he could count on was his Heavenly Father, Who held David tightly in His all-powerful hands.

No matter what happened to David in this life, God was in control. David also sought God's help to know the next steps he should take.

Do you have this assurance of God's love? Do you search for His will and direction for your daily steps? If not, let me invite you to seek Him out. He always has the answers and is always ready to welcome you in. God never fails to love us.

HOW DO YOU SPEND YOUR MORNINGS? DO YOU MAKE TIME FOR GOD AND HIS WORD?

DAY 144

"O LORD, what is man that you care for him, the son of man that you think of him? Man is like a breath; his days are like a fleeting shadow."

~*~

[A psalm of David, giving God glory for his successes and seeking His help to defeat his enemies.]

Have you ever looked up at the stars and been overwhelmed by the awe and majesty of the great heavenly expanse? Makes one feel quite small, doesn't it?

David was reflecting on how minute and insignificant humankind really is compared to an all-knowing, all-present God.

He asked God the why questions. Why do You care? What is it about man that makes You think of us? For we are just a vapor, here today and gone tomorrow, but You, Lord, are the Alpha and Omega, the beginning, and the end.

And you know what God's response was? John 3:16: "For God so loved the world that he gave his one and only Son, that whoever believes in him shall not perish but have eternal life."

God is a relational God. He desires to walk in close fellowship with each of us and loved us so much He died on a cross in our place. Now that is love.

WHAT WORDS DOES GOD SING OVER YOU? HOW DOES HE ENCOURAGE YOU IN YOUR DAILY WALK WITH HIM?

DAY 145

PSALM 145:8

"The LORD is gracious and compassionate, slow to anger and rich in love."

~*~

[A psalm of David giving praise to God for all He is and does for His Kingdom, His providence, etc.]

David is exuberant over the Lord and all His ways, throughout this psalm. And, in this one verse, we learn so much about our God…David's God.

First, the Lord is gracious. He is kind and generous of spirit. Even when we have been nothing but unloving and unappreciative of all He has provided for us, God offers His hand of fellowship and love.

Second, He is compassionate. God is not some distant mystical power. No, He is personal, up close and involved in our day-to-day lives.

He has walked this earth and understands our trials, temptations, and pain, therefore, He comes to our aid when we find ourselves in a pit of despair.

Third, God is slow to anger. Oh, but how we deserve His wrath, yet, He lingers, holding back with great restraint His indignation upon mankind so as many as possible may be saved. May we not tarry.

Finally, God is rich in love. Like a loving Father, He longs to bless His children with good things, and He delights in their joy. And because He loved you and me so much, He made the ultimate sacrifice so we could live. We are truly the ones who are rich!

HOW HAS GOD SHOWN YOU HIS GREAT COMPASSION?

DAY 146

"He upholds the cause of the oppressed and gives food to the hungry. The LORD sets prisoners free, the LORD gives sight to the blind, the LORD lifts up those who are bowed down, the LORD loves the righteous. The LORD watches over the alien and sustains the fatherless and the widow, but he frustrates the ways of the wicked."

~*~

[A Hallelujah psalm which teaches us to put our faith in God, not man, and gives a list of actions attributed to God.]

In these verses, the psalmist makes a list of things the Lord does for His creation, such as: upholding the cause of the oppressed, providing food for the hungry, giving sight to the blind, lifting up the broken, etc.

God shows no favoritism among mankind. It does not matter to Him what title or social status we have. He is there for those who are weak and overlooked. He loves to show up for the ones who have lost all hope. God is a God of mercy and compassion, and, like a Good Shepherd, He will pursue to the ends of the earth those who are lost and searching for a way out.

God is also a great comfort to those who have lost their spouse and to orphans. He lifts them, heals their wounds, and consoles their hearts. God will not, however, allow the wicked to get away with their deeds. He frustrates their plans and turns their schemes upon their own heads.

The Lord is actively involved in our lives but in turn, He requires our obedience, love, and loyalty. Small things, in my opinion, for such a great return!

DO YOU KNOW SOMEONE WHO HAS LOST THEIR SPOUSE OR PARENT(S)? WHAT CAN YOU DO TO SHOW THEM GOD'S LOVE?

DAY 147

PSALM 147:3-5

"He heals the brokenhearted and binds up their wounds. He determines the number of the stars and calls them each by name. Great is our LORD and mighty in power; his understanding has no limit."

~*~

[A psalm of praise of the Father who cares for the hurting, the insignificant, and the ill-forgotten.]

In these three verses the psalmist paints a beautiful picture of our God.

First, for those who have felt the sting of death or have lost their hope through some unfortunate circumstance, as the Great Physician, God begins the healing process by addressing the situation and binding the wounds.

Next, this personal and intimate Father is also the same uncontainable God who spoke the universe into existence, flung the stars across the expanse of the sky, and named them one by one. Nothing is too complex or vast for Him!

Finally, the psalmist shares his exuberance in praise for God because God's power and knowledge have no limit. There is no other like Him...none who can compare.

So, as the psalmist states in verse 1, "Praise the LORD. How good it is to sing praises to our God, how pleasant and fitting to praise him!" May we all reiterate and agree. Yes, indeed, praise the Lord!

HAVE YOU LOOKED AT THE STARS LATELY? ISN'T IT MIND BLOWING TO KNOW THAT GOD HAS THEM ALL NAMED AND THAT HE HAS THAT SAME CARE FOR YOU?

DAY 148

PSALM 148:13

"Let them praise the name of the LORD, for his name alone is exalted; his splendor is above the earth and the heavens."

~*~

[A call to every creature on the earth, to praise the Lord, from the exalted to the lowly. For God's name alone is to be exalted.]

All I could do was sit and sing praises to God. My husband and I had travelled to Wyoming for a conference where I was teaching. On the morning we had a long break, we visited Devil's Tower, an impressive butte in the Black Hills. After climbing up to the base of it, I sat and looked out over the beautiful valley below. There was something worshipful in the air. I could not help but to sing praises to God for His majesty and holiness.

What more can be said? The psalmist, in this verse, has invited all creation to sing the praises of our God and King, for He alone is worthy.

No other being is responsible for measuring out the heavens or laying the foundations of the earth. No one can take credit for breathing life into all living beings or giving His own life as an atoning sacrifice. And our own bodies? They are so uniquely designed that if our DNA could be stretched out and measured, it would reach from planet Earth to Pluto and back, a whopping 10 billion or so miles! THAT is our God![15]

The majesty of God's glory cannot be contained even unto the highest heavens, for He outshines even His most intricate handiwork.

Today, don't take for granted or fail to acknowledge God's magnificence, His holiness, and the splendor of His might, for there truly is no other like our God!

HOW CAN YOU WORSHIP GOD TODAY? WHAT THINGS WILL YOU THANK HIM FOR?

---

[15] "91 Amazing Human Body Facts," Karin Lehnardt, https://www.factretriever.com/body-facts.

DAY 149

PSALM 149:4-5

"For the LORD takes delight in his people; he crowns the humble with salvation. Let the saints rejoice in this honor and sing for joy on their beds."

~*~

[A song of jubilation, sang at the coming of the Lord. A song of triumph over His enemies.]

God takes great delight in His people as they serve Him by making them more like Christ through their worship, in their prosperity, in their humility, etc., God cares for and relishes in His faithful followers.

In times of various trials, He sets the crown of victory upon their head, but He also leads those who have a humble and seeking heart to salvation and eternal rest.

Those who have had a life-changing encounter with God, cannot *not* talk about Him. They rejoice at the great and awesome things He has done, and even on their beds or in their private quiet place, must sing His praises, for He has never failed them.

As we close out this day, let us, too, give God all the praise He deserves because His delight is in His children, therefore, He clothes them with holiness and love.

DO YOU PRAY AND THANK GOD WHEN YOU LIE DOWN AT NIGHT? IF NOT, WHY NOT TRY IT THIS EVENING?

DAY 150

PSALM 150:6

"Let everything that has breath praise the LORD. Praise the LORD."

~*~

[The last psalm in the collection and one full of praise! The psalmist closes this text with thirteen "Praise the Lord! Praise him, phrases. It is the rally cry of the book.]

Don't you love a great ending to a movie? When everything turns out right in the end...guy gets the girl...good trumps evil?

As we conclude our Psalm journey, it is only fitting for the last one to be full of adoration and praise.

The psalmist begins by praising God in His sanctuary; in His mighty heavens; for His acts of power and surpassing greatness. He then transfers over to praising God with all the musical instruments, i.e., trumpet, harp, lyre, cymbals, etc.

Finally, the psalmist ends with verse 6 as a charge to all: "Let everything that has breath praise the LORD."

Why should we praise? Because when we

acknowledge our love and appreciation for God and all He is and has done for us, our prayer takes our minds off ourselves and places our thoughts on the rightful focus of our worship—Him. It helps us to remember who we are and Who God is.

My prayer is you, the reader, have received encouragement and hope from this journey. God is so worthy of our praise, and I think we see the Psalms display the importance of making time for Him; learning how to be still; seeking after and praising Him. God bless you, friend, and Praise the Lord!

HOW WILL YOU CONTINUE THIS JOURNEY OF PRAISE?

Thank you

We appreciate you reading this Crossover Books title.
For other titles, please visit our on-line bookstore at
www.pelicanbookgroup.com.

For questions or more information, contact us at
customer@pelicanbookgroup.com.

Crossover Books is
an imprint of Pelican Book Group
www.PelicanBookGroup.com

Connect with Us
www.facebook.com/Pelicanbookgroup
www.twitter.com/pelicanbookgrp

To receive news and specials, subscribe to our bulletin
http://pelink.us/bulletin

May God's glory shine through
this work of fiction.

AMDG

You Can Help!

At Pelican Book Group it is our mission to entertain readers with fiction that uplifts the Gospel. It is our privilege to spend time with you awhile as you read our stories.

We believe you can help us to bring Christ into the lives of people across the globe. And you don't have to open your wallet or even leave your house!

Here are 3 simple things you can do to help us bring illuminating fiction™ to people everywhere.

1) If you enjoyed this book, write a positive review. Post it at online retailers and websites where readers gather. And share your review with us at reviews@pelicanbookgroup.com (this does give us permission to reprint your review in whole or in part.)

2) If you enjoyed this book, recommend it to a friend in person, at a book club or on social media.

3) If you have suggestions on how we can improve or expand our selection, let us know. We value your opinion. Use the contact form on our web site or e-mail us at customer@pelicanbookgroup.com

God Can Help!

Are you in need? The Almighty can do great things for you. Holy is His Name! He has mercy in every generation. He can lift up the lowly and accomplish all things. Reach out today.

Do not fear: I am with you; do not be anxious: I am your God. I will strengthen you, I will help you, I will uphold you with my victorious right hand.

~Isaiah 41:10 (NAB)

We pray daily, and we especially pray for everyone connected to Pelican Book Group—that includes you! If you have a specific need, we welcome the opportunity to pray for you. Share your needs or praise reports at http://pelink.us/pray4us

Free eBook Offer

We're looking for booklovers like you to partner with us! Join our team of influencers today and periodically receive free eBooks!

For more information
Visit http://pelicanbookgroup.com/booklovers

How About Free Audiobooks?

We're looking for audiobook lovers, too! Partner with us as an audiobook lover and periodically receive free audiobooks!

For more information
Visit
http://pelicanbookgroup.com/booklovers/freeaudio.html

or e-mail
booklovers@pelicanbookgroup.com

www.ingramcontent.com/pod-product-compliance
Lightning Source LLC
Chambersburg PA
CBHW022115080426
42734CB00006B/137